16 Caprices
for Solo Violin
Op. 4

Composed and Illustrated by Michael Tseitlin

Published by CAMUS

ISBN: 978-0-557-12515-9

Manufactured in the United States

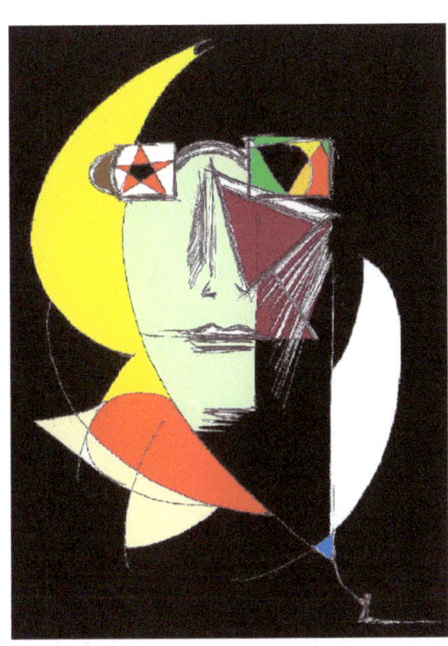

I sketched out 24 Caprices between September 10th and 20th, 2008. Then I forgot about them until about February 2009 when I decided to finish 16 of them.

Each caprice is dedicated to a colleague, former or present student, or a family member. As an artist, writer, and composer, I had an opportunity to illustrate my music. Some music and pictures are bizarre, some funny and some sad, but all followed the same principle as all my music and art: it has a meaning.

Some of the caprices have been composed to be paired with some well known concertos. The last three caprices (No. 14, 15, and 16) can be used as cadenzas to Paganini's Concerto No. 1, Vieuxtemps' Concerto No. 5 and Beethoven's Concerto.

All caprices should be played very freely and musically. I encourage performers to create their own music and not to be afraid of being disrespectful to the composer (in this case, me). Physically all caprices should be played with extremely relaxed hands. That is how they work best.

Michael Tseitlin May 14, 2009

Self-Portrait, 2008. Pencil on Paper, colored on computer

Index of Music and Art

No. 1 "Widmung" is dedicated to my former student, wonderful violinist, winner of many international competitions, Professor at Juilliard School of Music, and Concertmaster of the Metropolitan Opera Orchestra David Chan.
Art: "Widmung"pencil and ink on paper.
No. 2 "Ten Letters" is dedicated to my former student, child prodigy and present violinist with the Metropolitan Opera Orchestra Yurika Mok. Art: "View" pencil on paper, colored on computer.
No. 3 "High Noon Storm" is dedicated to my dear teacher at Gnesin's Institute and current Professor at the Royal Academy of Music in London Felix Arkadievich Andrievsky. His teaching inspired and enlightened my musical life for the rest of my days. I am forever grateful to him.
Art: "Abandoned City" pencil on paper, colored on computer
No. 4 On the Theme "Stars and Stripes Forever" or "Stretch your Imagination and Call Your Chiropractor" is dedicated to my dear friend and amazing violinist with great sense of humor, Professor at the University de Montreal Vladimir Landsman. Art: "Escape" pencil on paper, colored on computer.
No. 5 "Cold Night" is dedicated to my former student, violinist with great lyrical personality and wonderful, deep and expressive tone, Concertmaster of Rotterdam Philharmonic Igor Gruppman. Art: "Wedding" acrylic on canvas.
No. 6 "Corrida or Bull Fighting Chords" is dedicated to my former student, child prodigy with a gift for science, and childhood friend of my children Bertrand Yeung. Art: "Rage" pencil on paper, colored on computer.
No. 7 "Day in a park with Eva and butterflies" is dedicated to my grand daughter Eva and her mother Rebecca, fine violinist and dedicated teacher. Art: "Let's play" pencil on paper, colored on computer.
No. 8 "Taming the Ball" is dedicated to my former student, Professor at the California Institute of Music Tiffany Modell. Art: "Taming the Ball" pencil on paper, colored on computer.
No. 9 "Cell Phone Polka" is dedicated to my son Sasha, very creative violinist, violist, teacher and composer.
Art: "Prince of Shinjuku", pencil on paper, colored on computer.
No. 10 "Midnight Flight" is dedicated to a good friend and colleague, Professor at the Tokyo College of Music Masaoki Inoue. Art: "Night Flight", oil pastel on paper.
No. 11 "You Can Do It!" is dedicated to my former student residing in Germany, accomplished baroque violinist and dedicated teacher Paul Lindenauer. Art: "Circus", pencil on paper, colored on computer.
No. 12 "Midnight Serenade in style of Szymanowski" is dedicated to my son Pasha. An accomplished soloist, he loves music of Szymanowski and has a very special feeling for it. Art: "Adagio", pencil on paper, colored on computer
No. 13 "Youth and Incredible Lightness of Being in Taos" is dedicated to my former student, Concertmaster of Milwaukee Symphony, prize winner of Tchaikovsky and Paganini competitions Frank Almond. The title reflects on memories of several summers in Taos, New Mexico. Art: "Encore", pencil on paper, colored on computer.
No. 14 "Cadenza to the First Movement of Concerto No. 1 by N. Paganini" is dedicated to my 15 years old student Carolyn Lee for whom I wrote this cadenza when she studied the first concerto. Art: "Paganini", pencil on paper, colored on computer.
No. 15 "Cadenza to the First Movement of Concerto No. 5 by Vieuxtemps" is dedicated to my wife Irina. Her amazing sound and expressiveness of playing inspired this caprice, without coda, can be used as a cadenza to Concerto No. 5. Art: "Fighting the Dragon", acrylic on canvas.
No. 16 "Cadenza to Beethoven" is also dedicated to my wife Irina. Beethoven is her favorite concerto and I had a privilege to write 3 cadenzas for her when she was performing it in Portugal. Art: "Awakening", pencil and ink on paper.

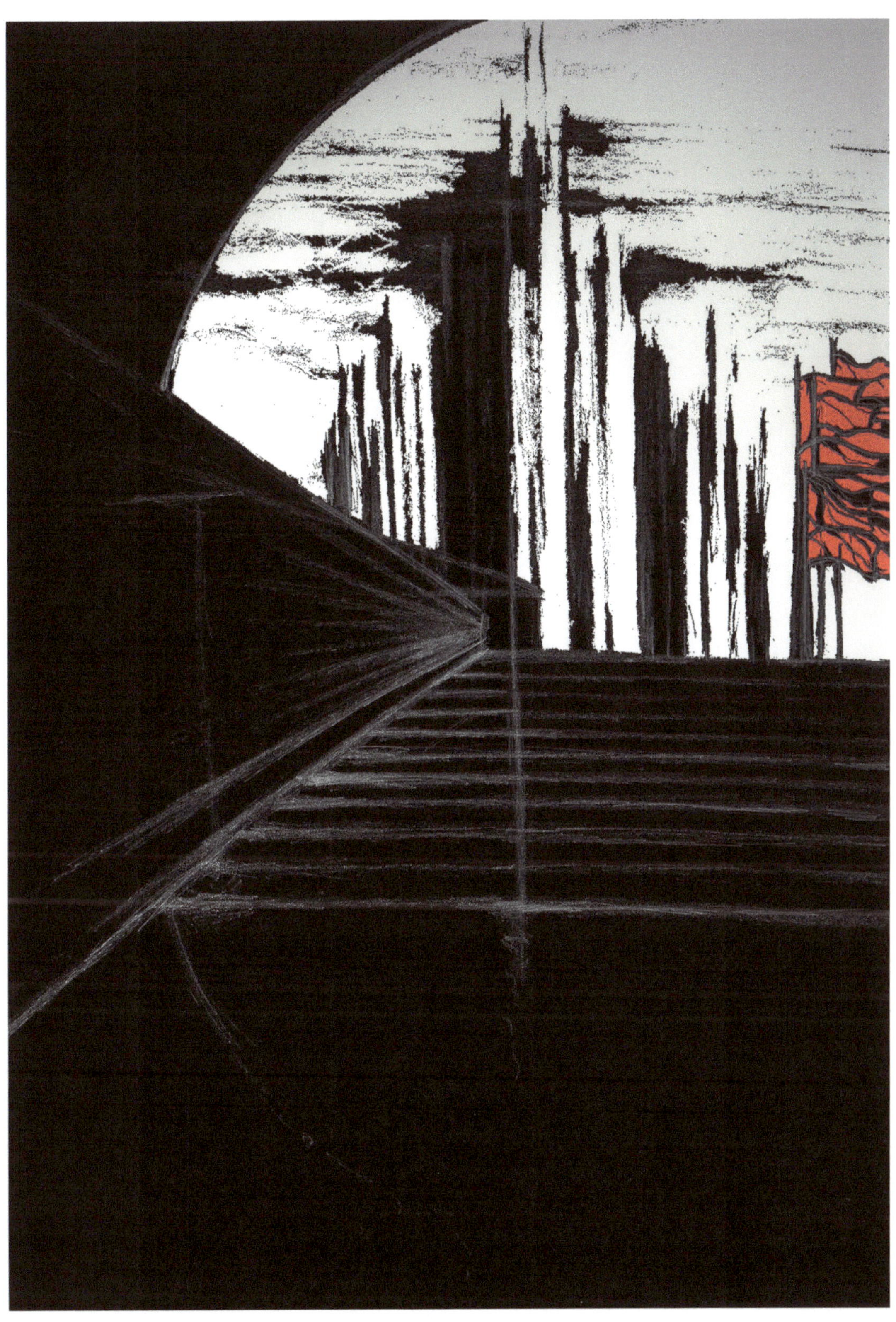

Castle with a Red Flag

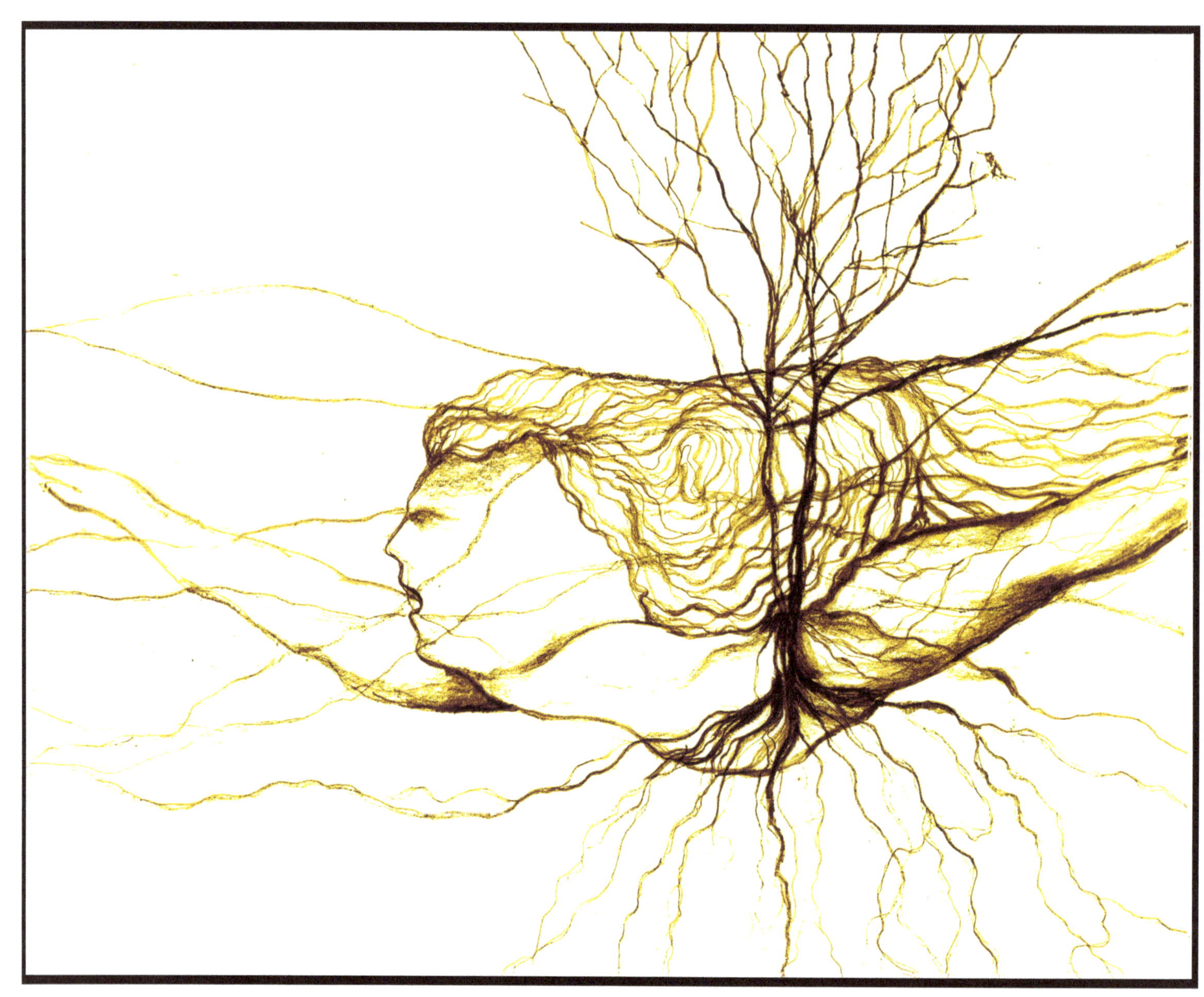

No. 1

Widmung

16 CAPRICES FOR SOLO VIOLIN, Op. 4

I. Widmung

To David Chan

Michael Tseitlin

Allegro molto ma grazioso

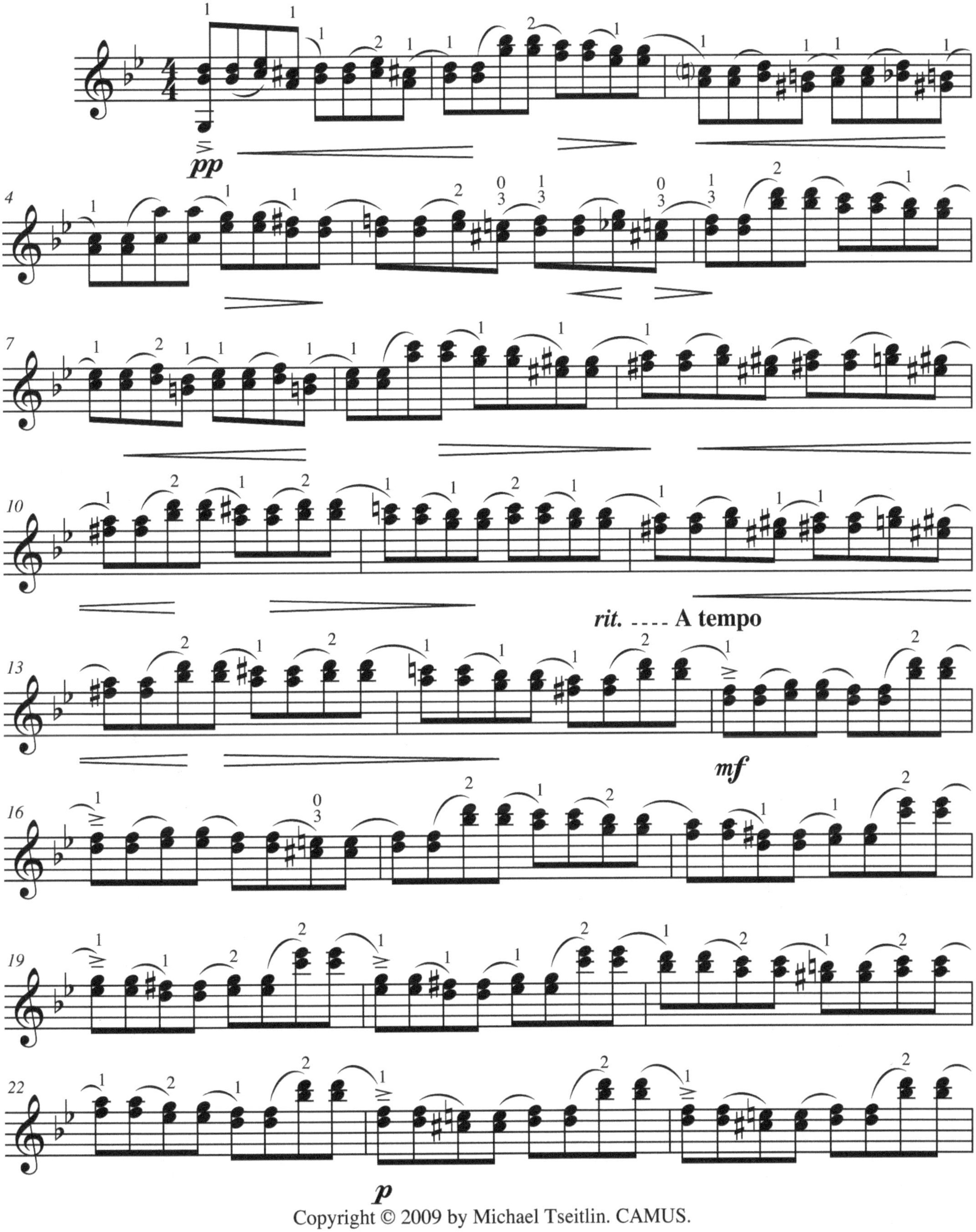

pp

rit. ---- **A tempo**

mf

p

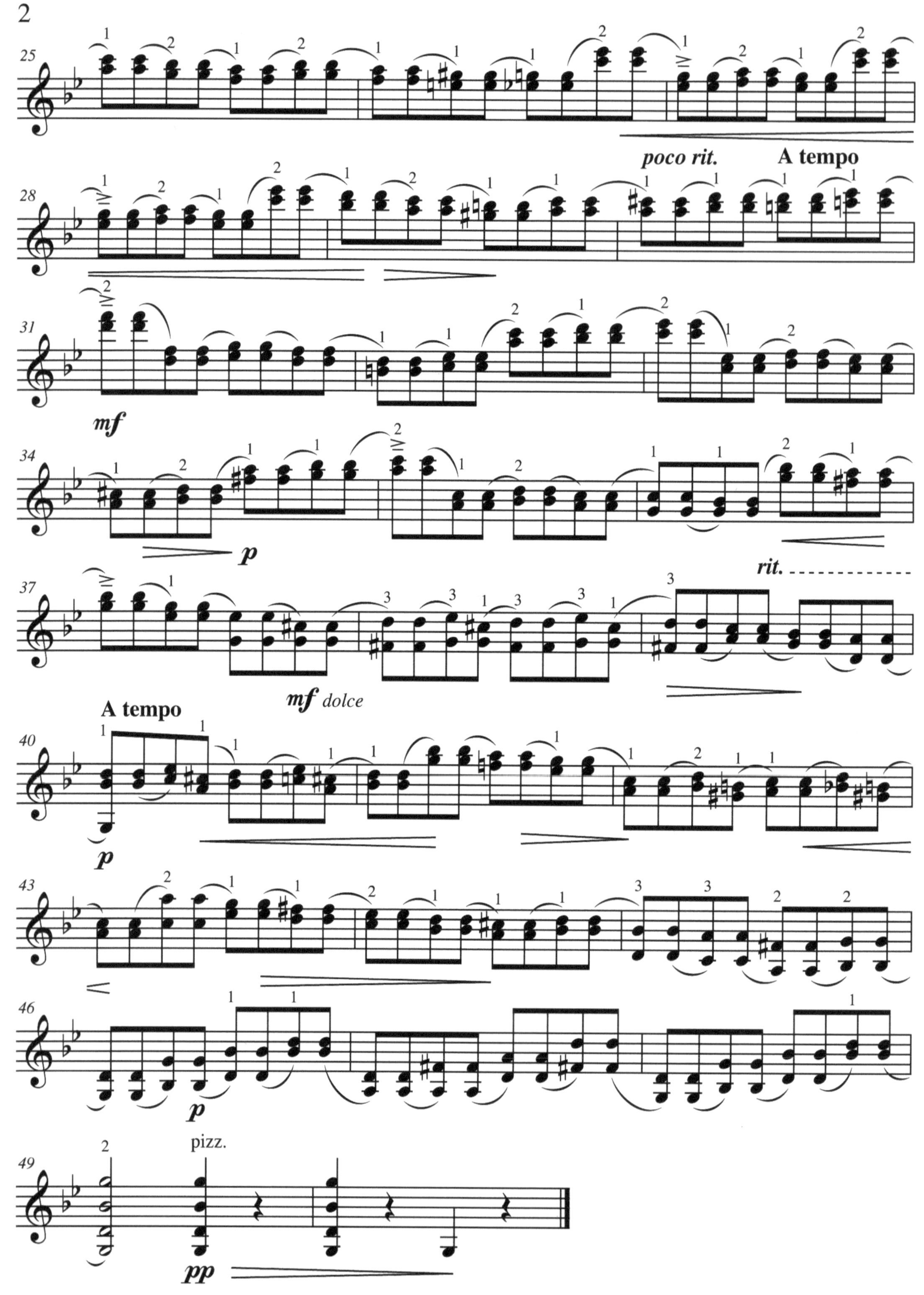
poco rit.
A tempo
mf
p
rit.
mf dolce
A tempo
p
p
pizz.
pp

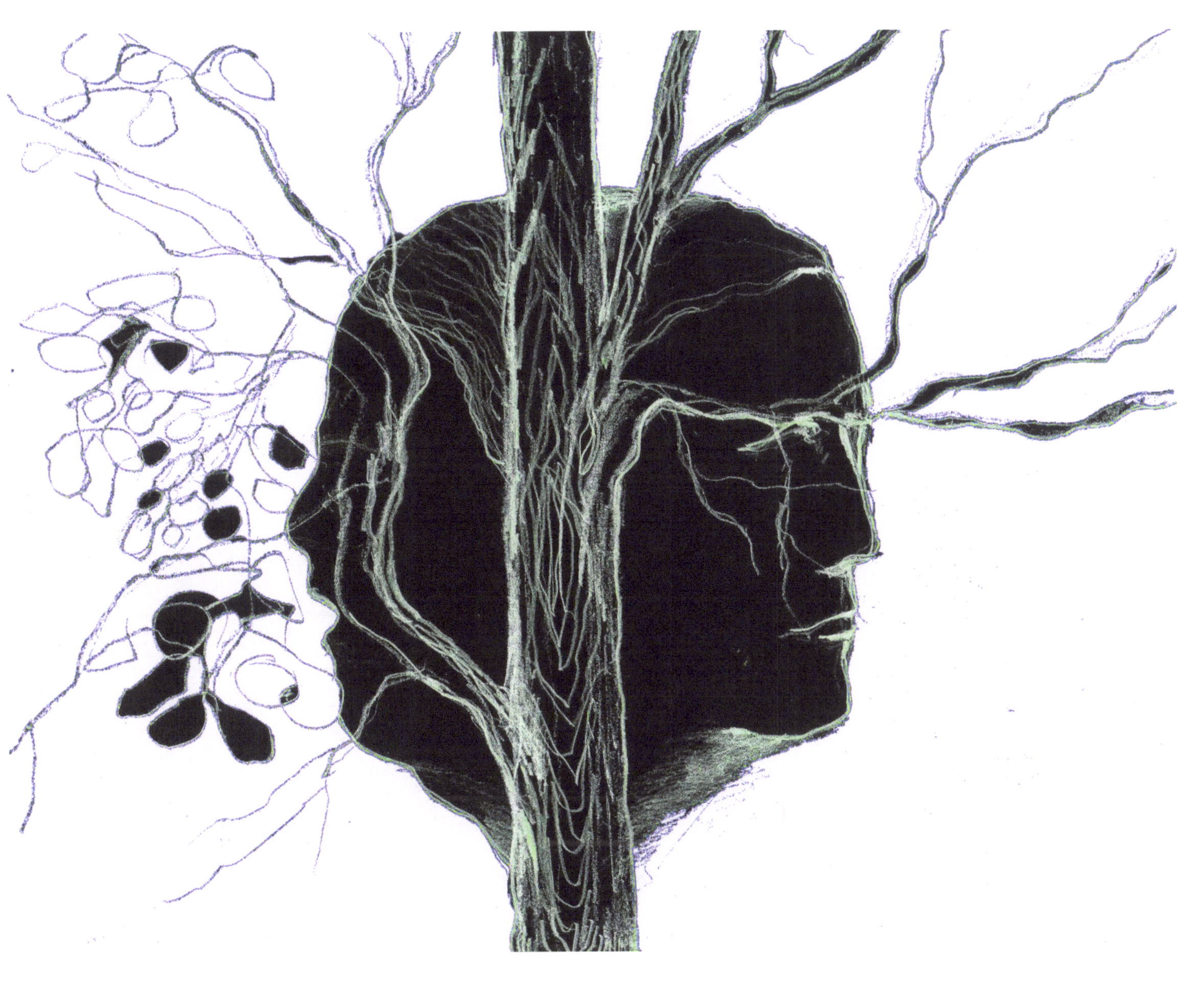

No. 2
Ten Letters

to Yurika Mok

II. 10 Letters in Tenths

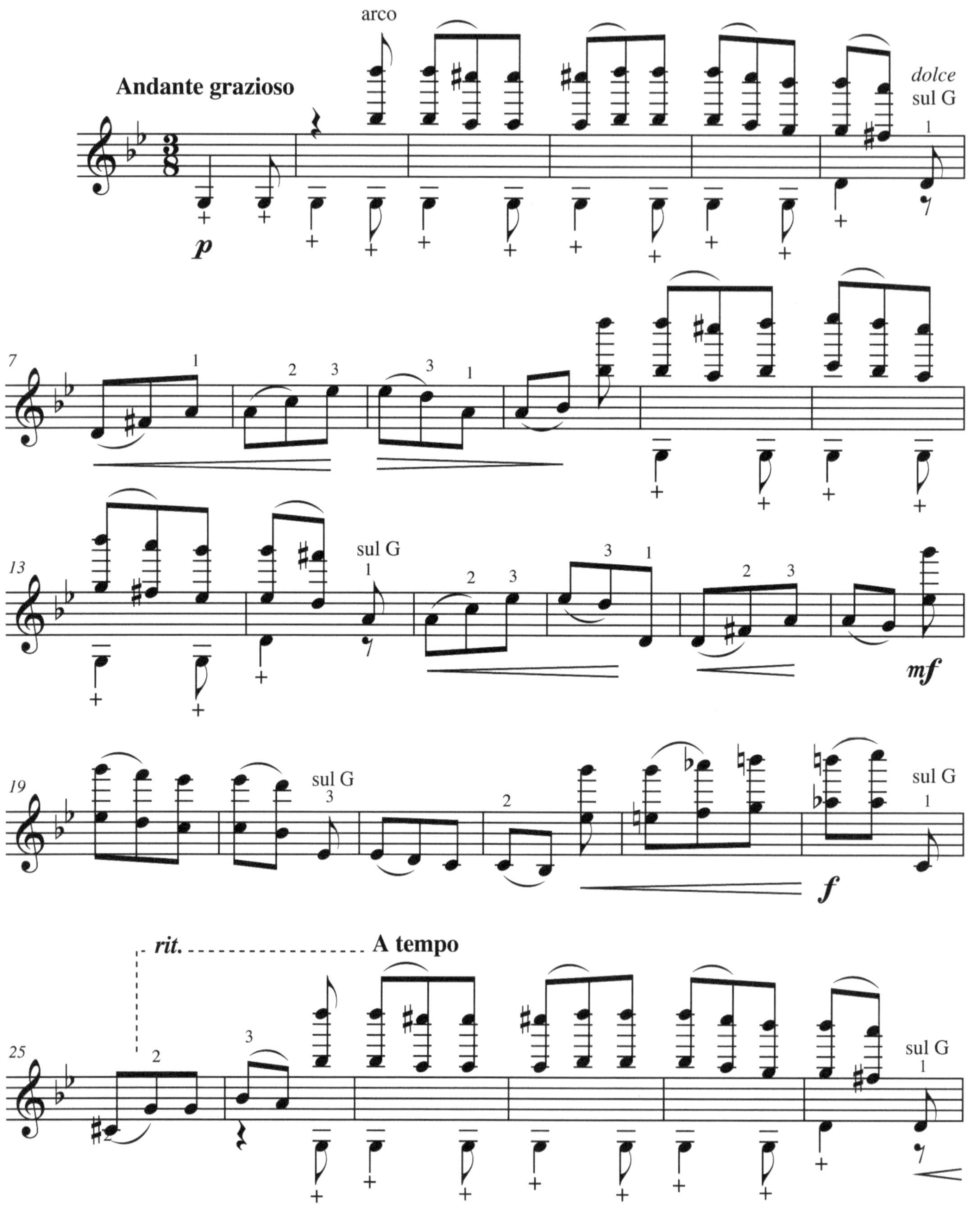

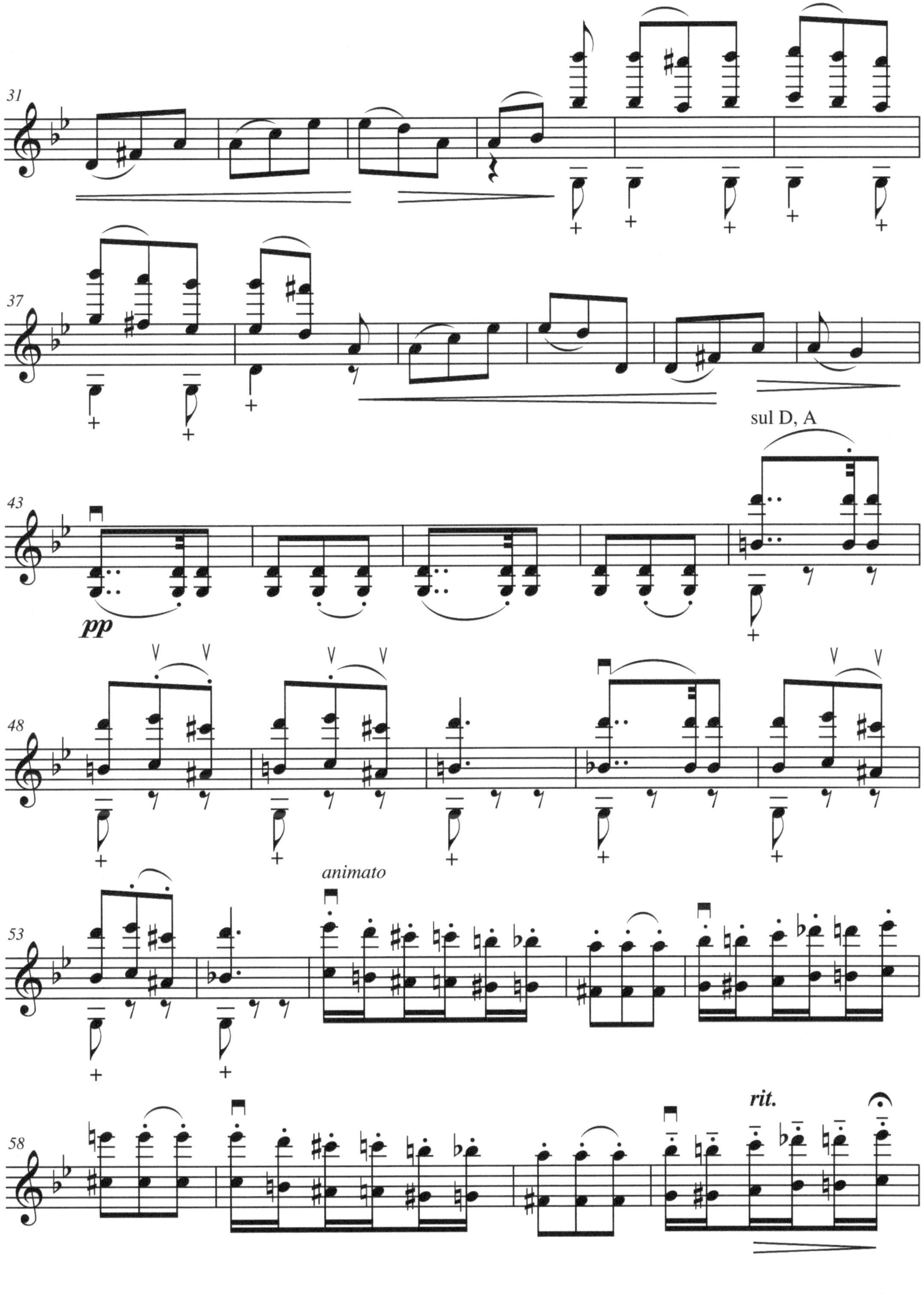

31

37

43 sul D, A

pp

48

53 *animato*

58 *rit.*

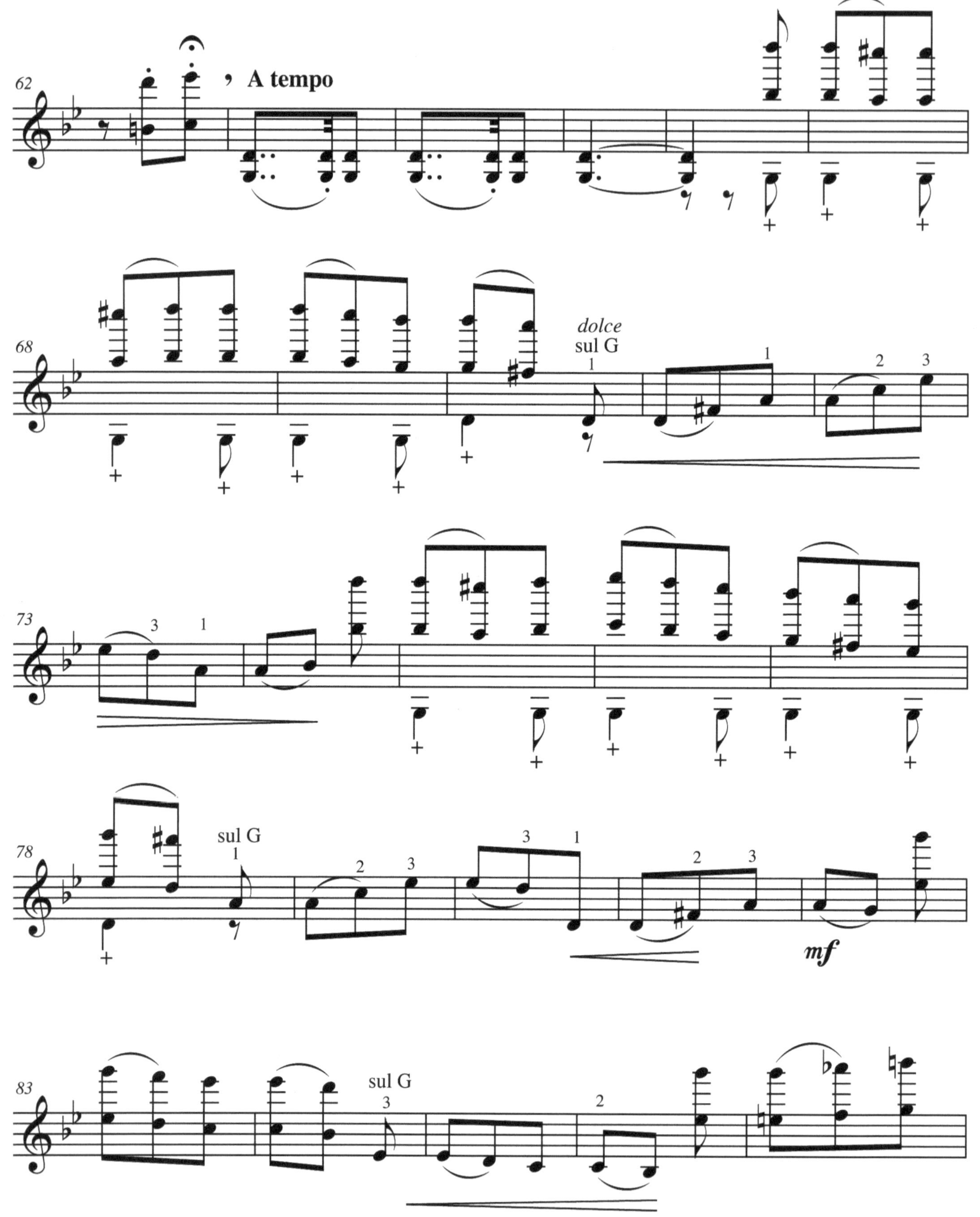
A tempo
dolce
sul G
sul G
mf
sul G

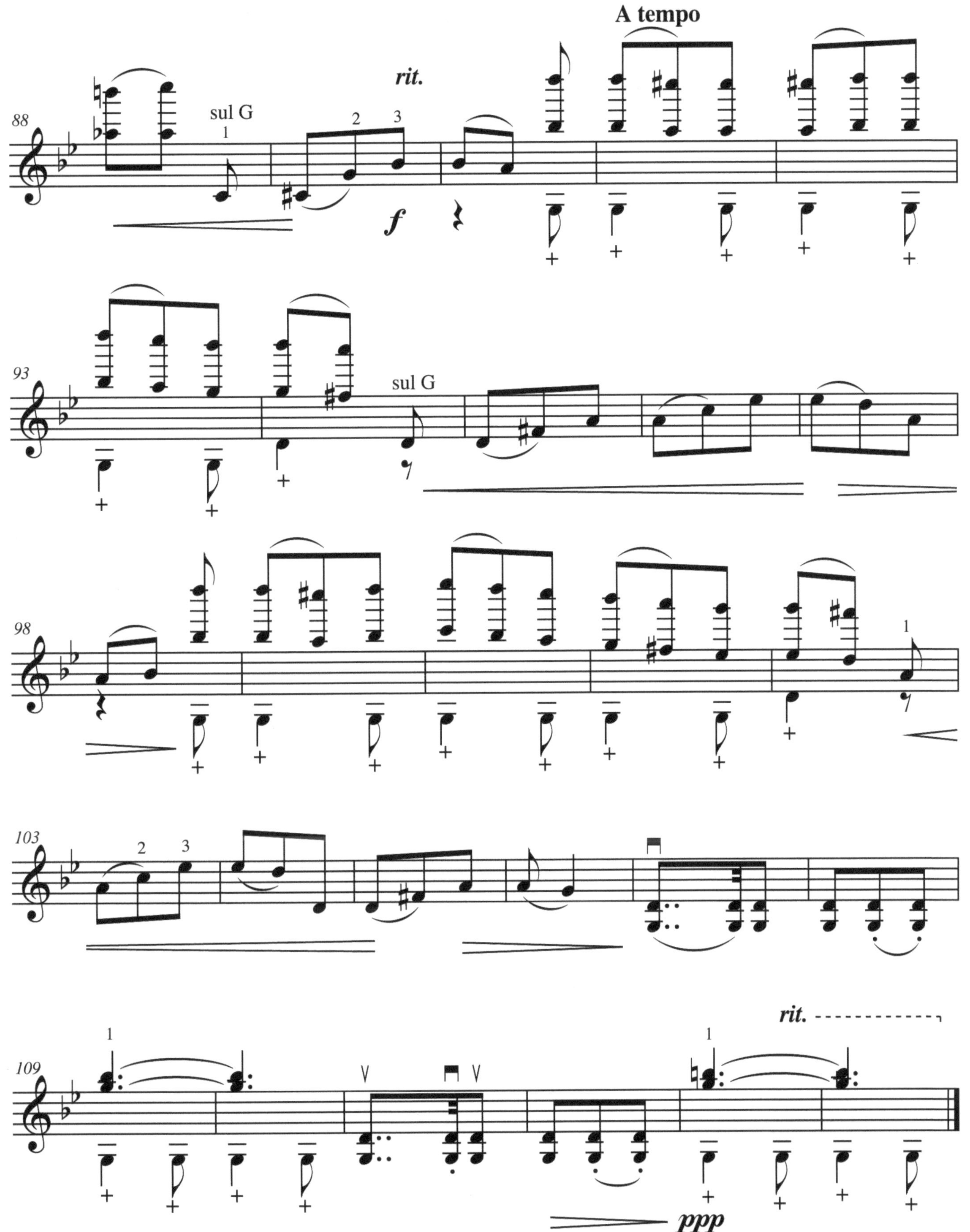
A tempo
rit.
88
sul G
f
93
sul G
98
103
109
rit.
ppp

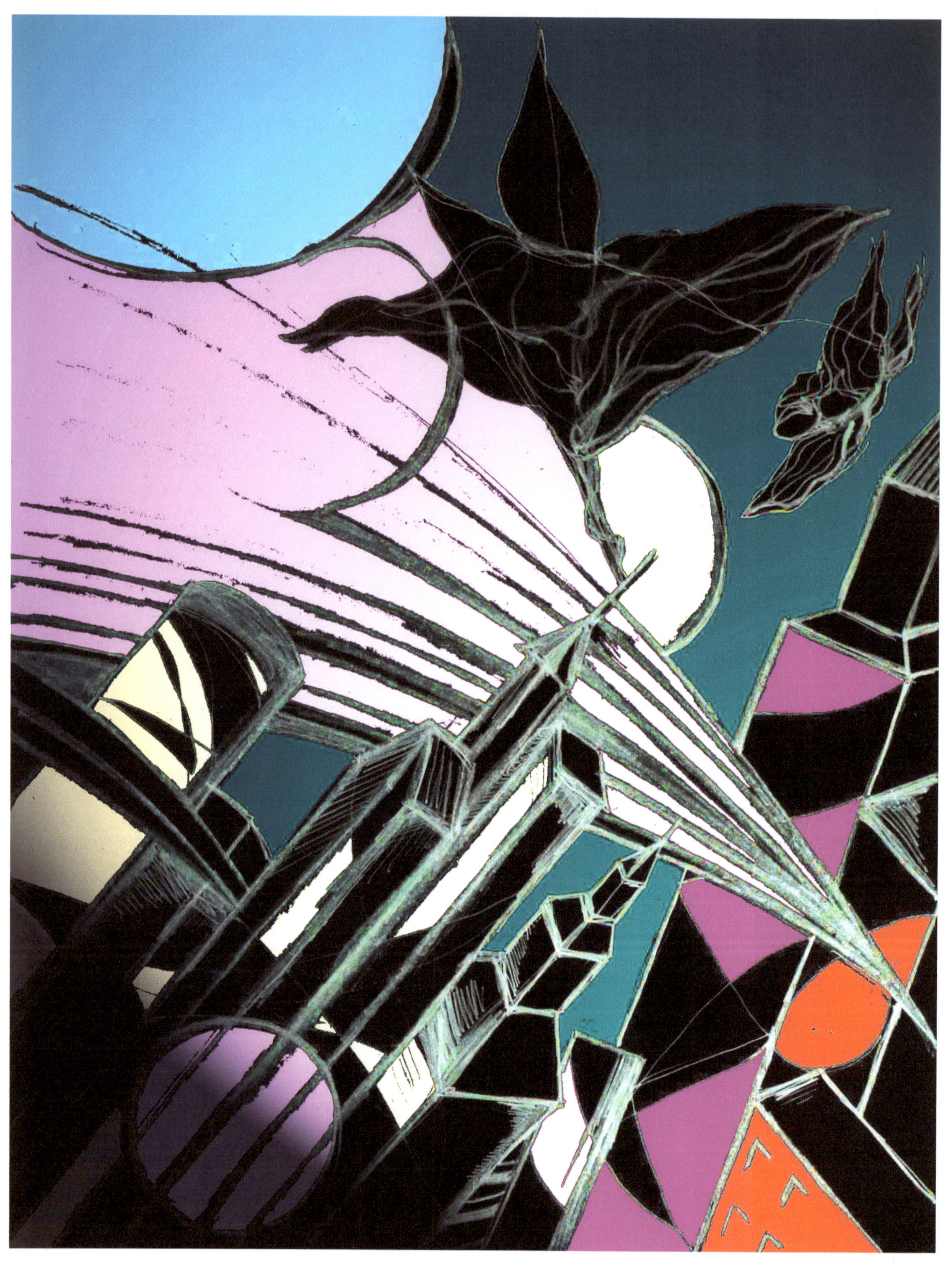

No. 3
High Noon Storm

to Felix Andrievsky

III. Sailing Uncharted Waters in High Noon Storm

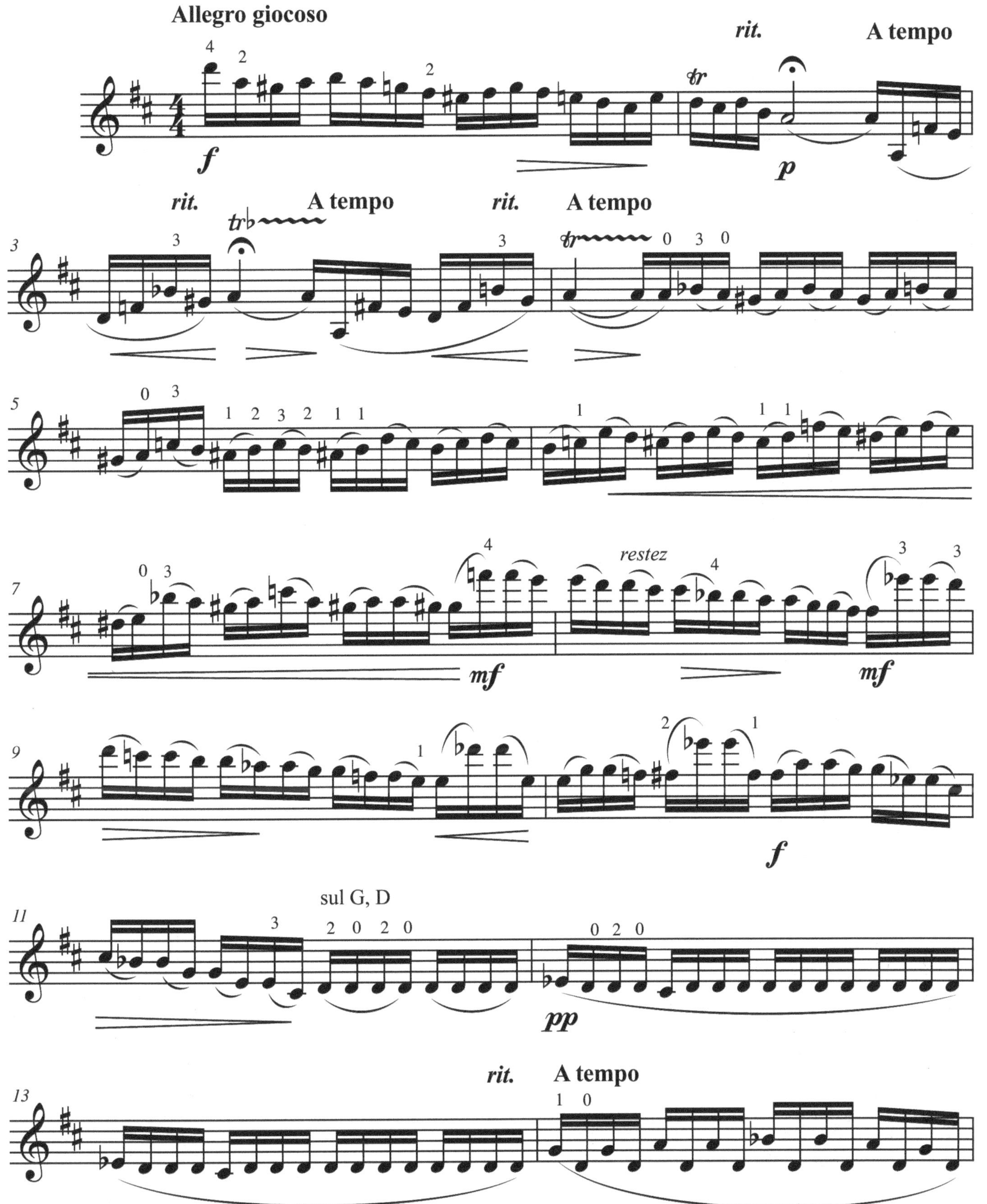

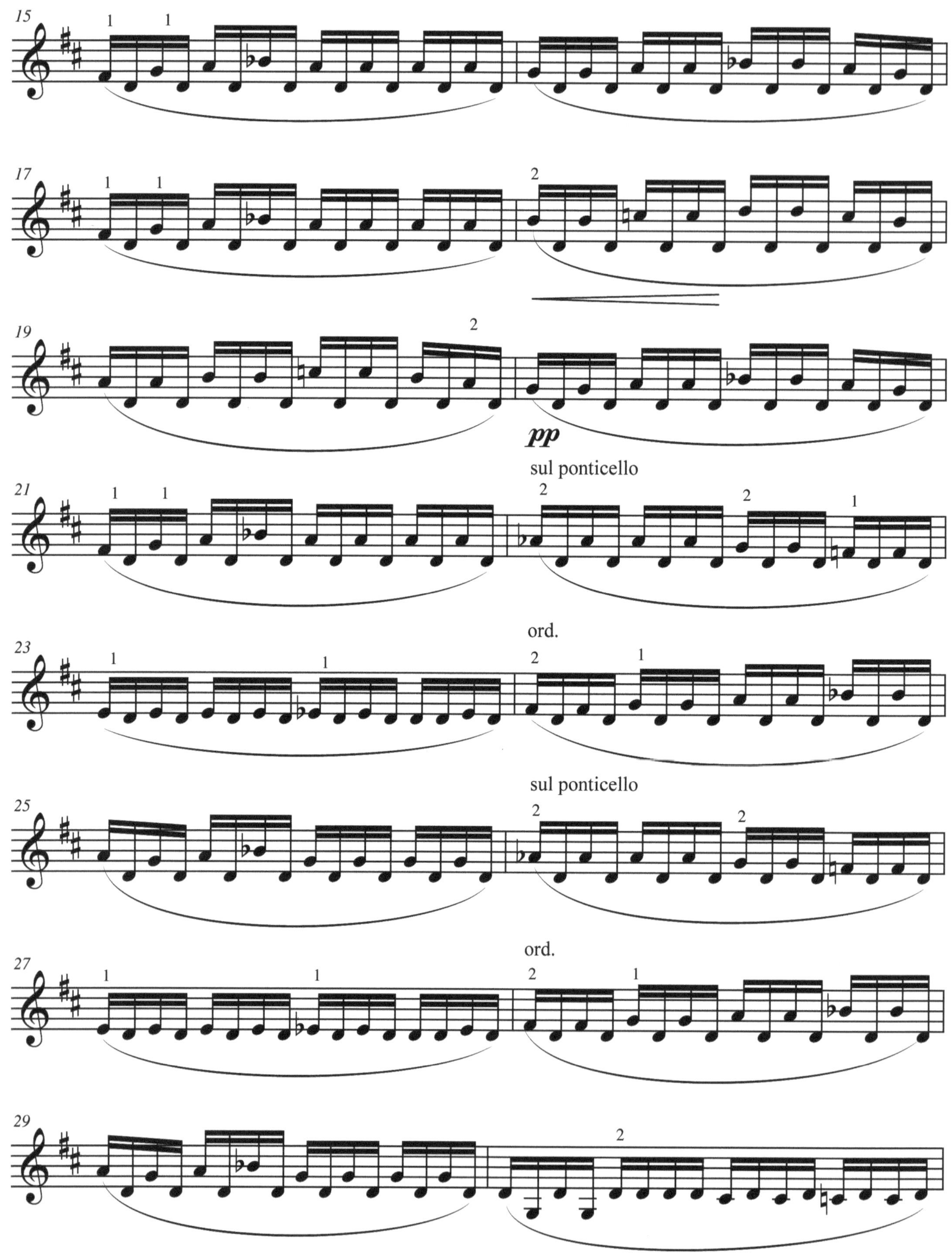
pp
sul ponticello
ord.
sul ponticello
ord.

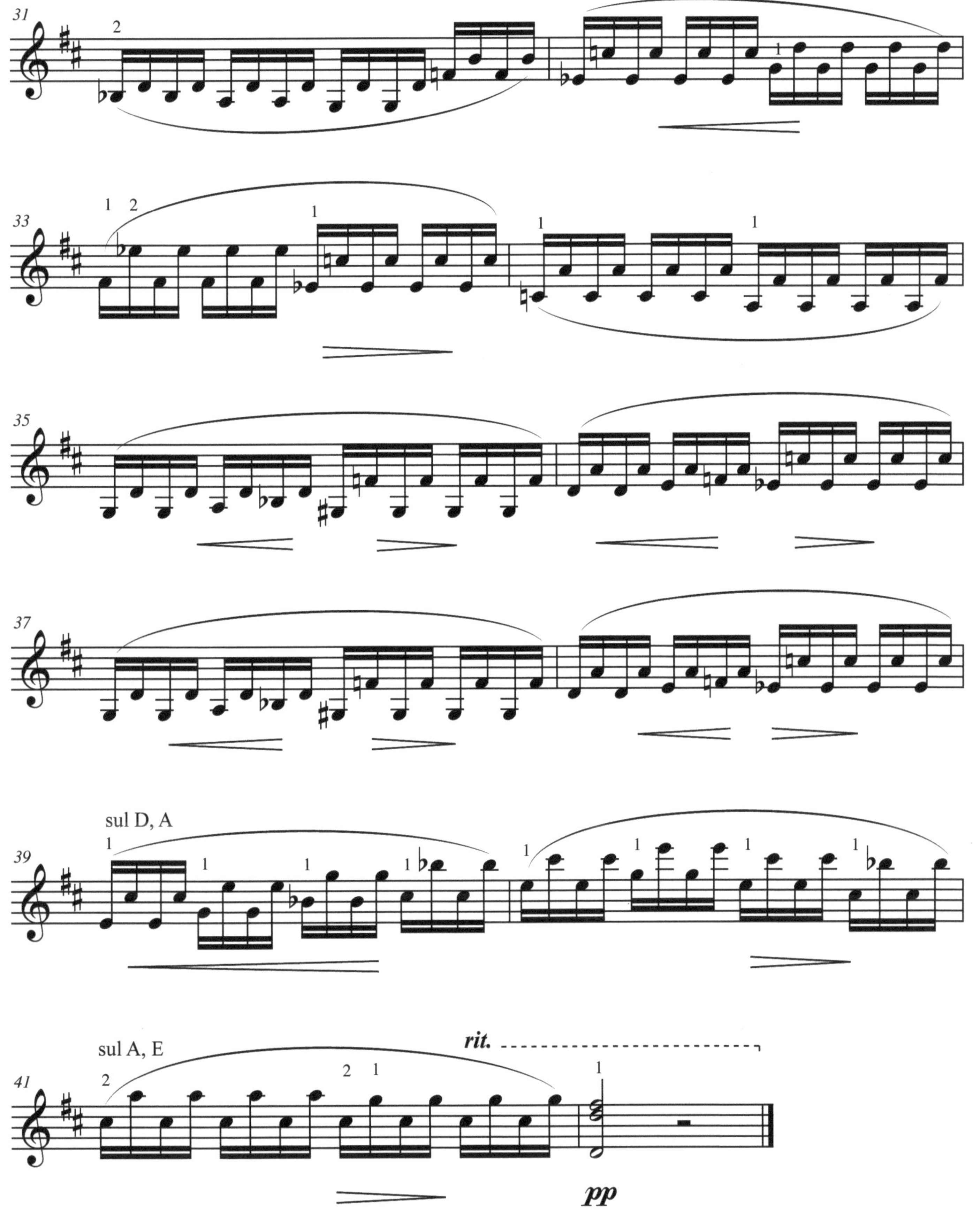
sul D, A
sul A, E
rit.
pp

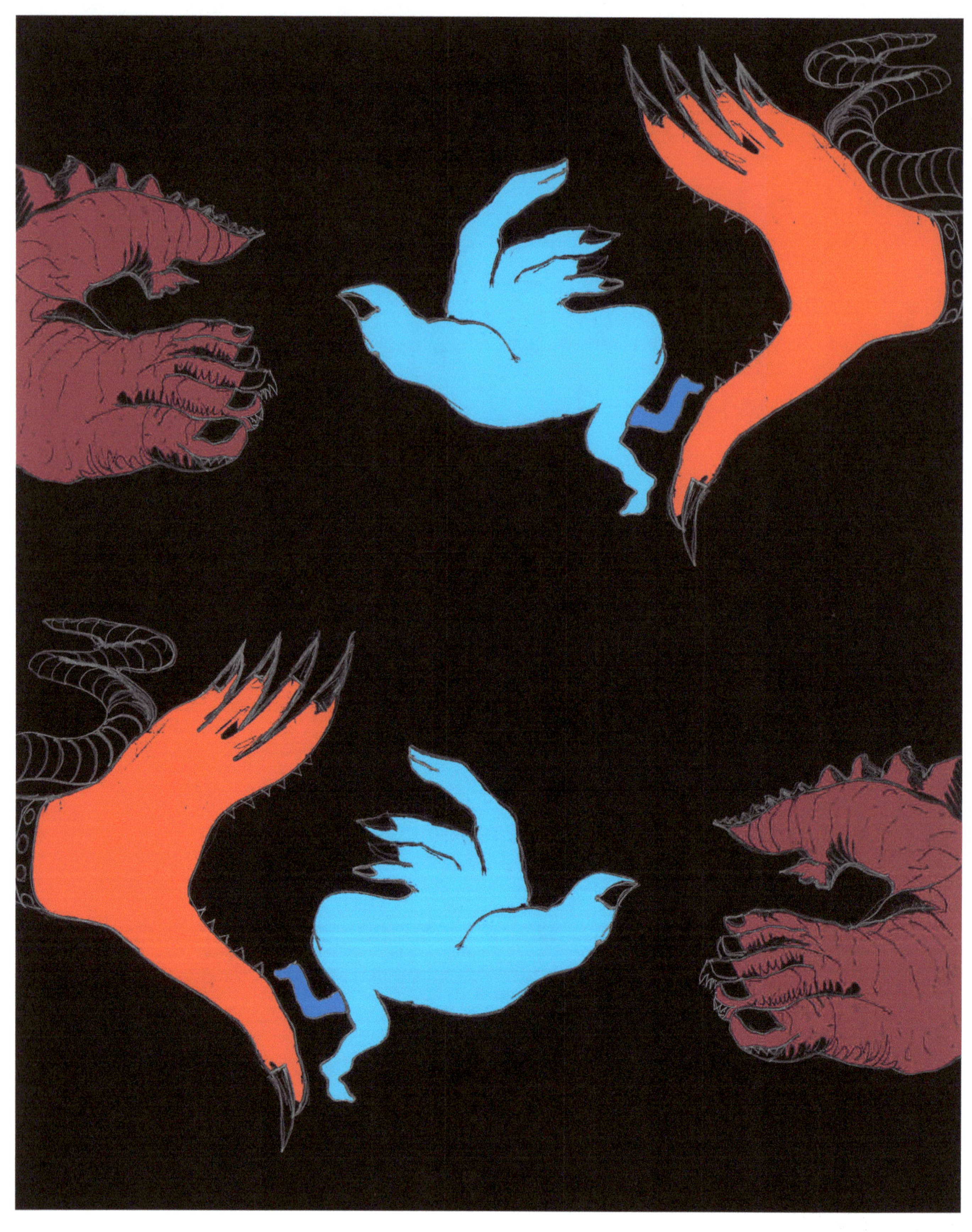

No. 4

On the Theme "Stars and Stripes Forever"

To Vladimir Landsman

IV. After the Theme "Stars and Stripes Forever" or "Stretch Your Imagination and Call Your Chiropractor"

Allegro con left hand spaghetti e prego, molto spiccato

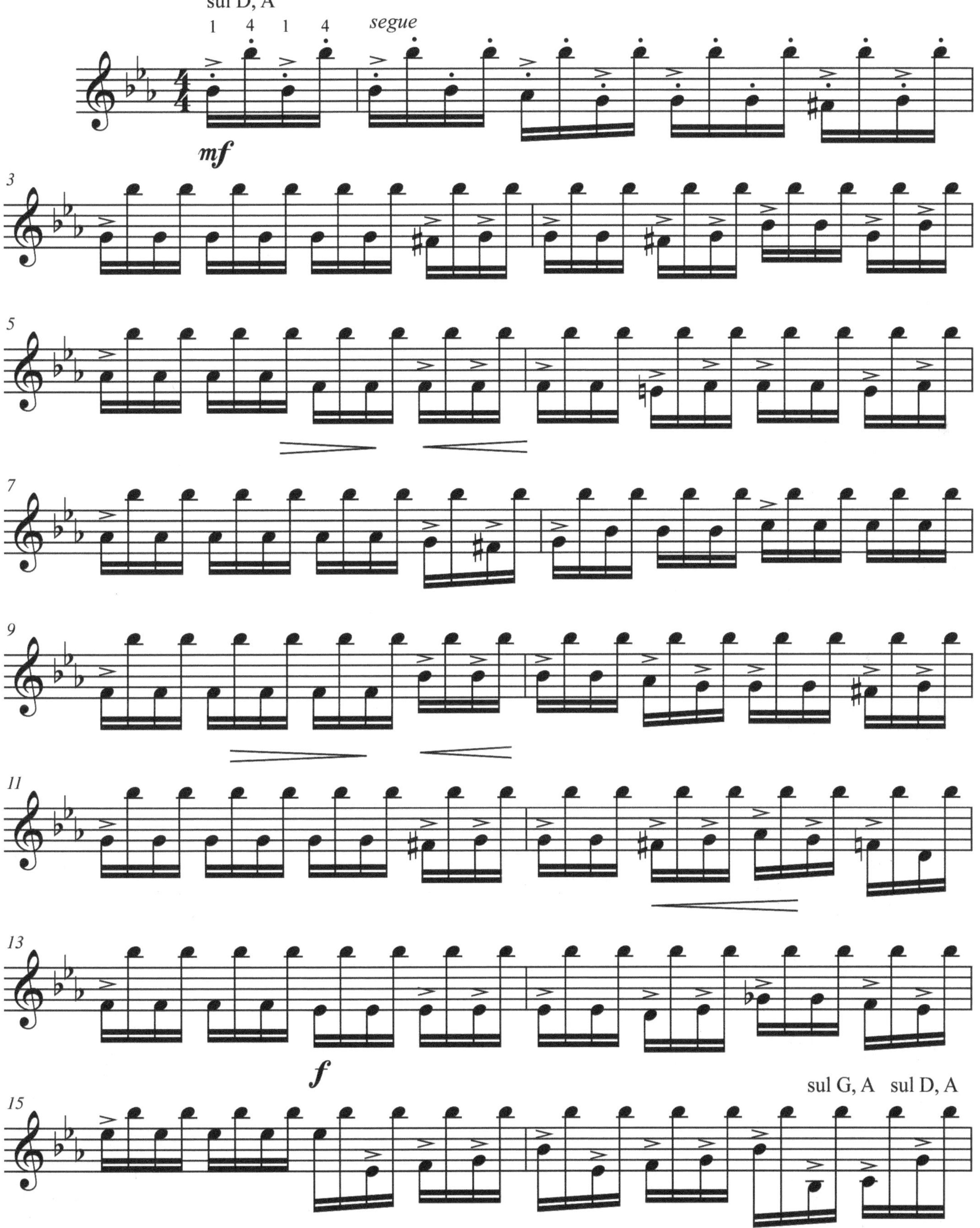

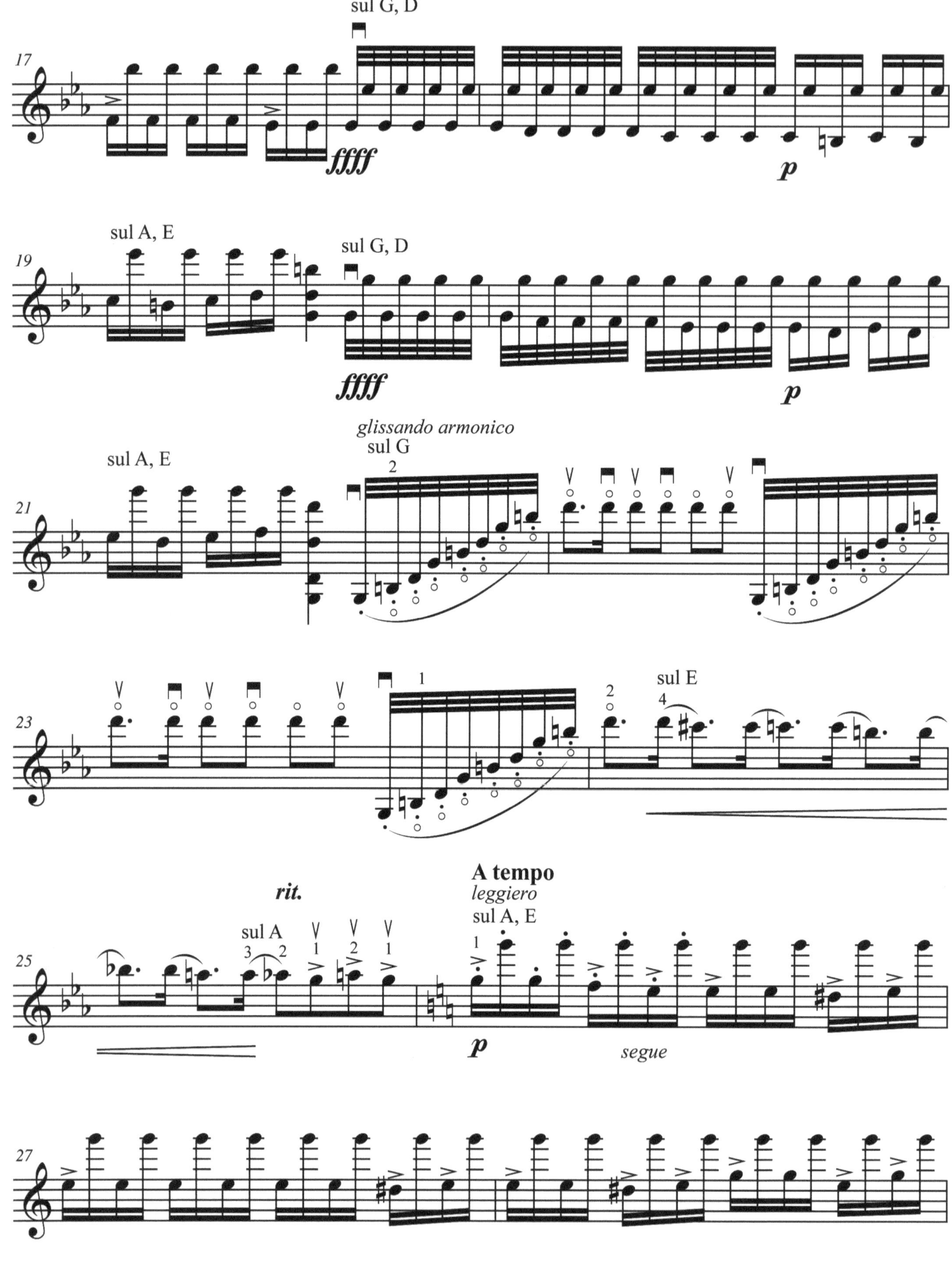
17
sul G, D
ffff
p
19
sul A, E
sul G, D
ffff
p
glissando armonico
sul G
21
sul A, E
23
sul E
25
rit.
sul A
A tempo
leggiero
sul A, E
p
segue
27

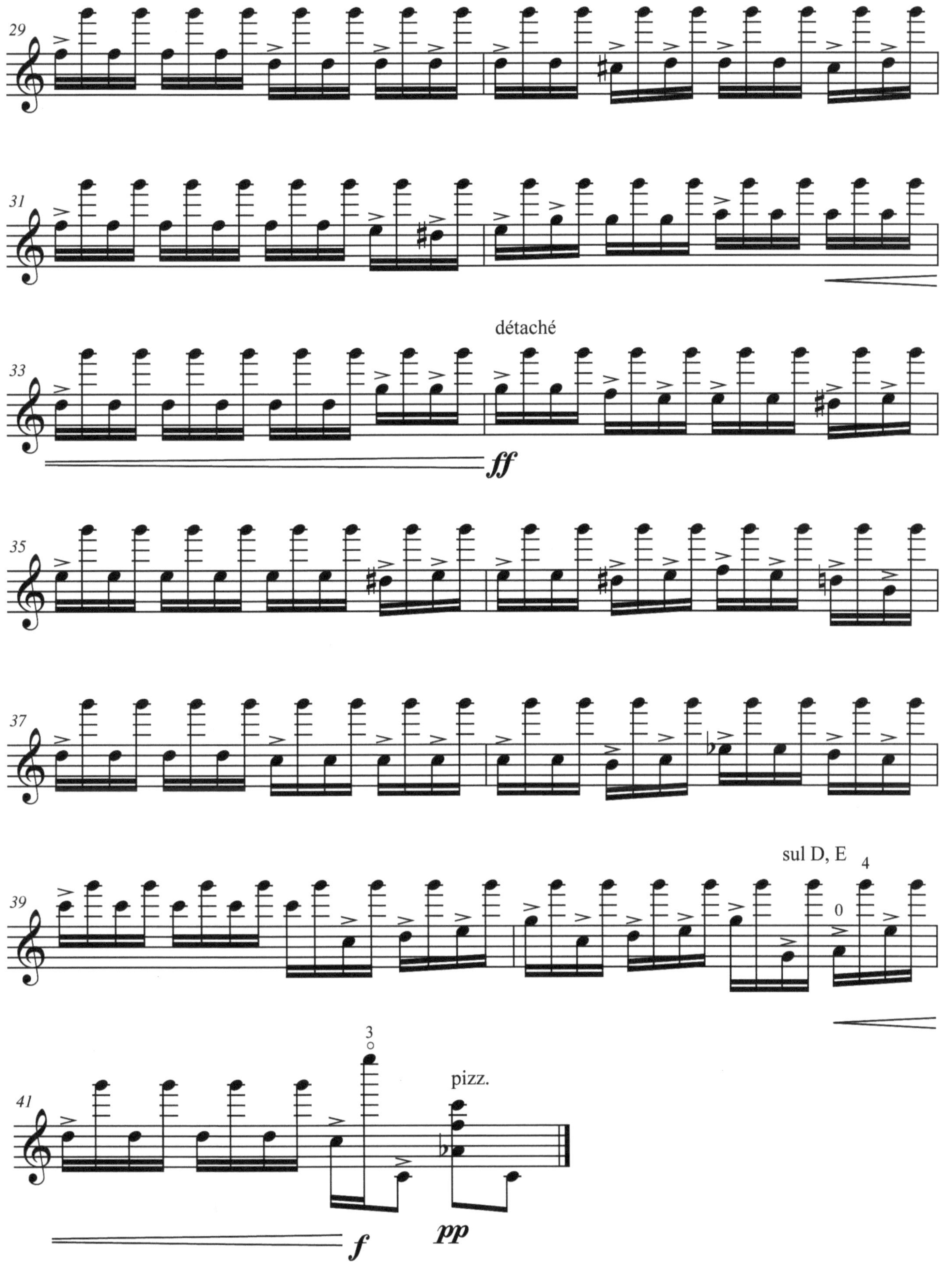

29
31
détaché
33
ff
35
37
sul D, E
4
0
39
3
pizz.
41
f
pp

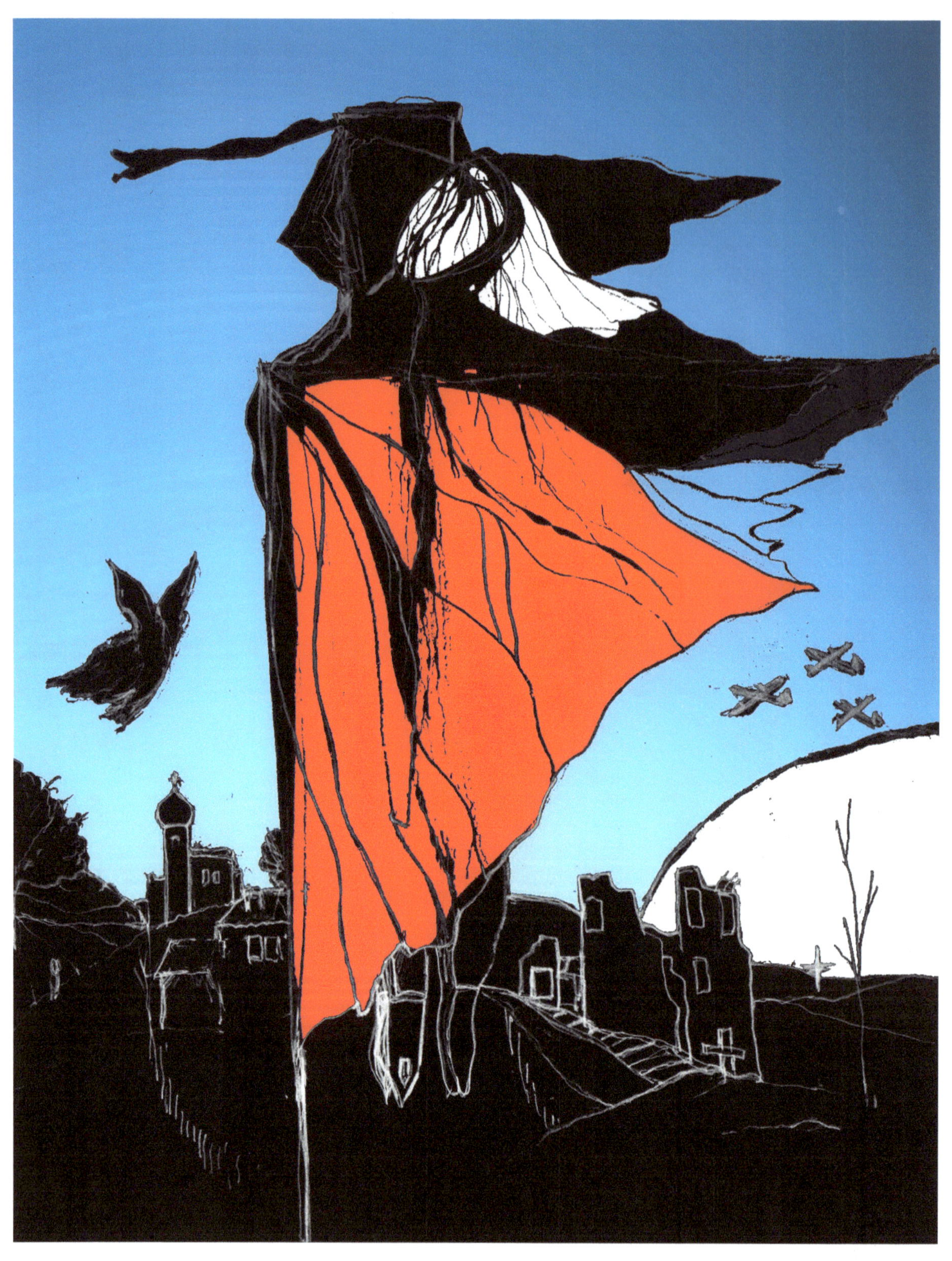

No. 5
Cold Night

To Igor Gruppman

V. Cold Night

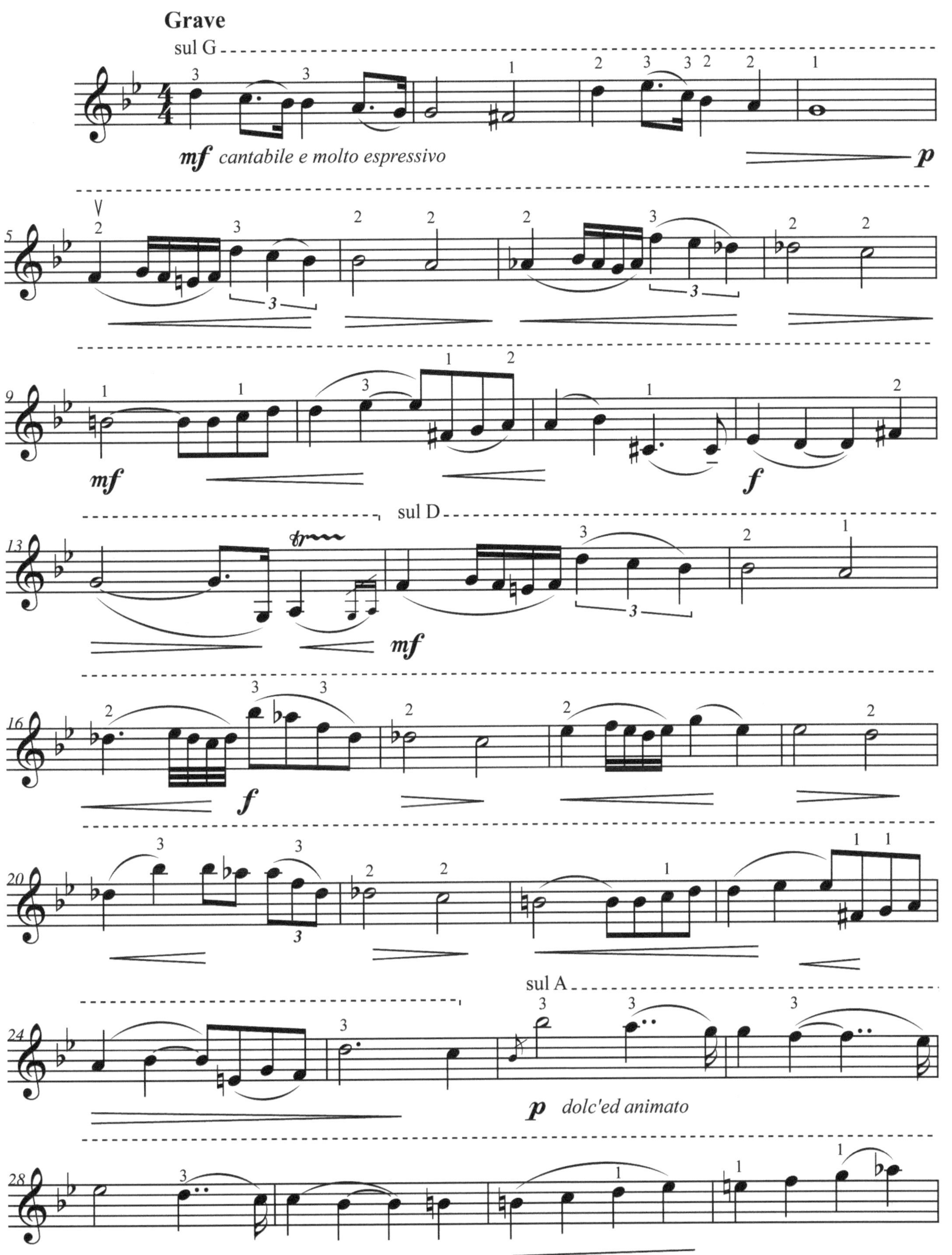

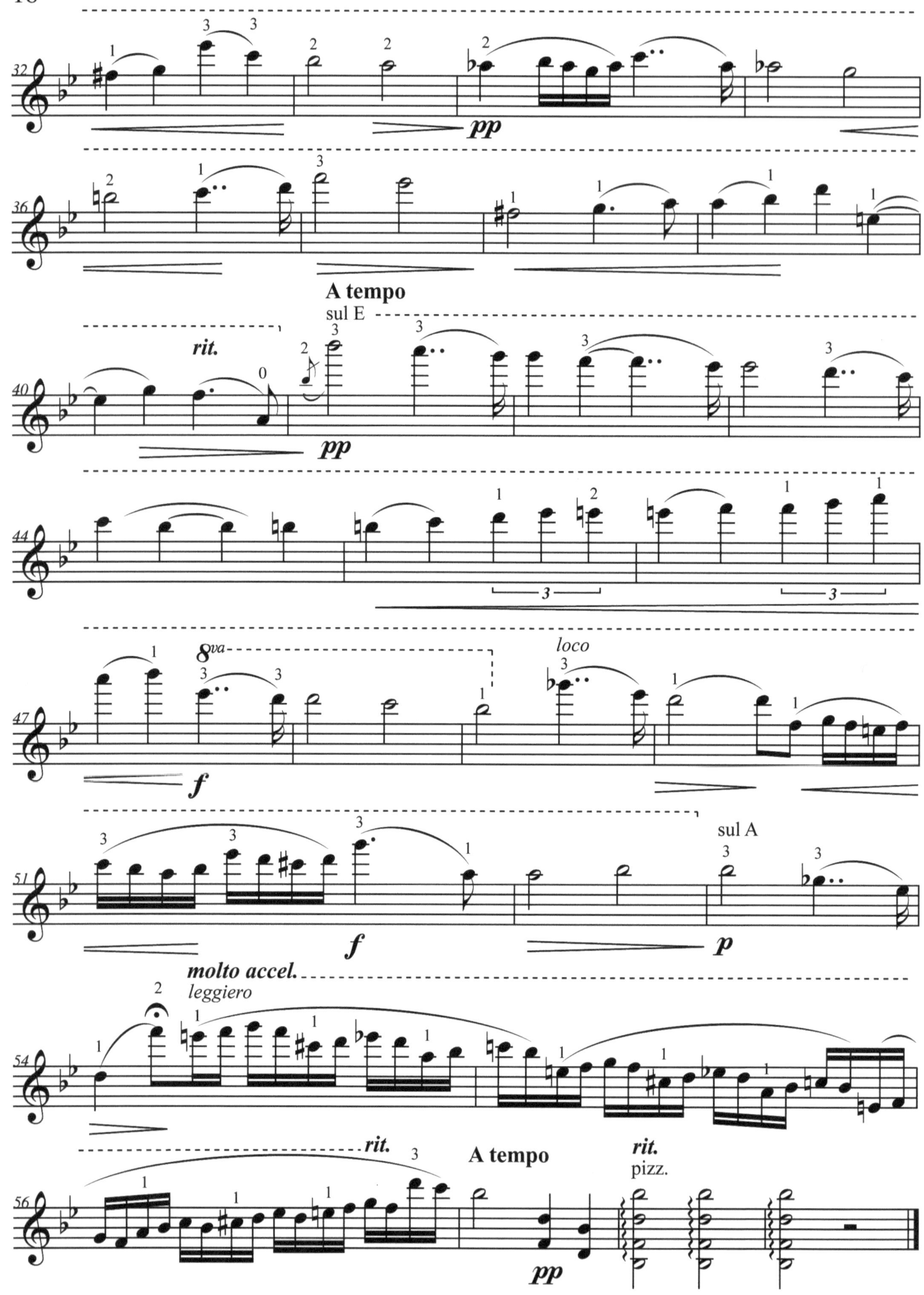
rit.
A tempo
sul E
8va
loco
sul A
molto accel.
leggiero
rit.
A tempo
rit.
pizz.

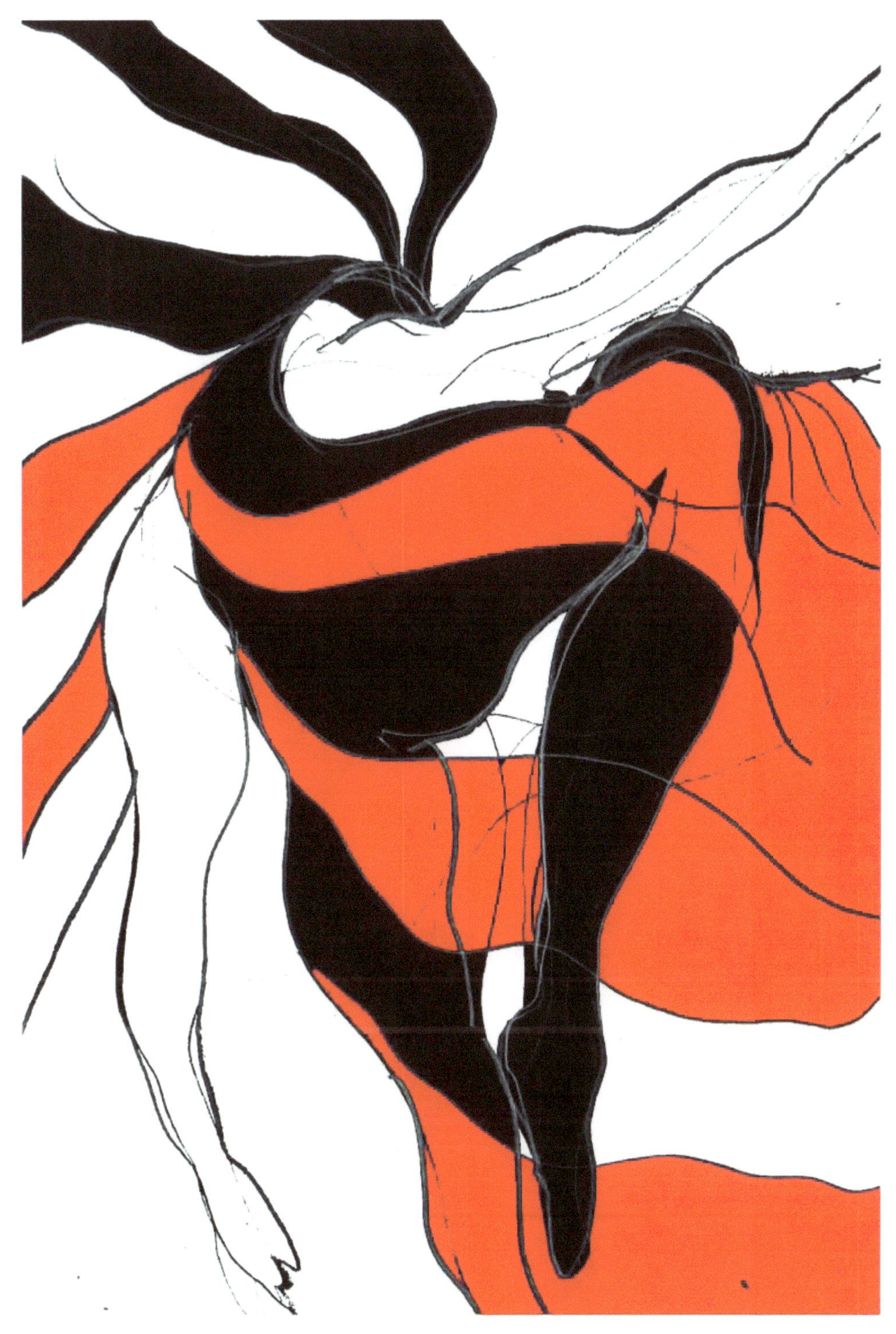

No. 6

Corrida
Bull Fighting Cords

To Bertrand

VI. Corrida or Bull Fighting Chords

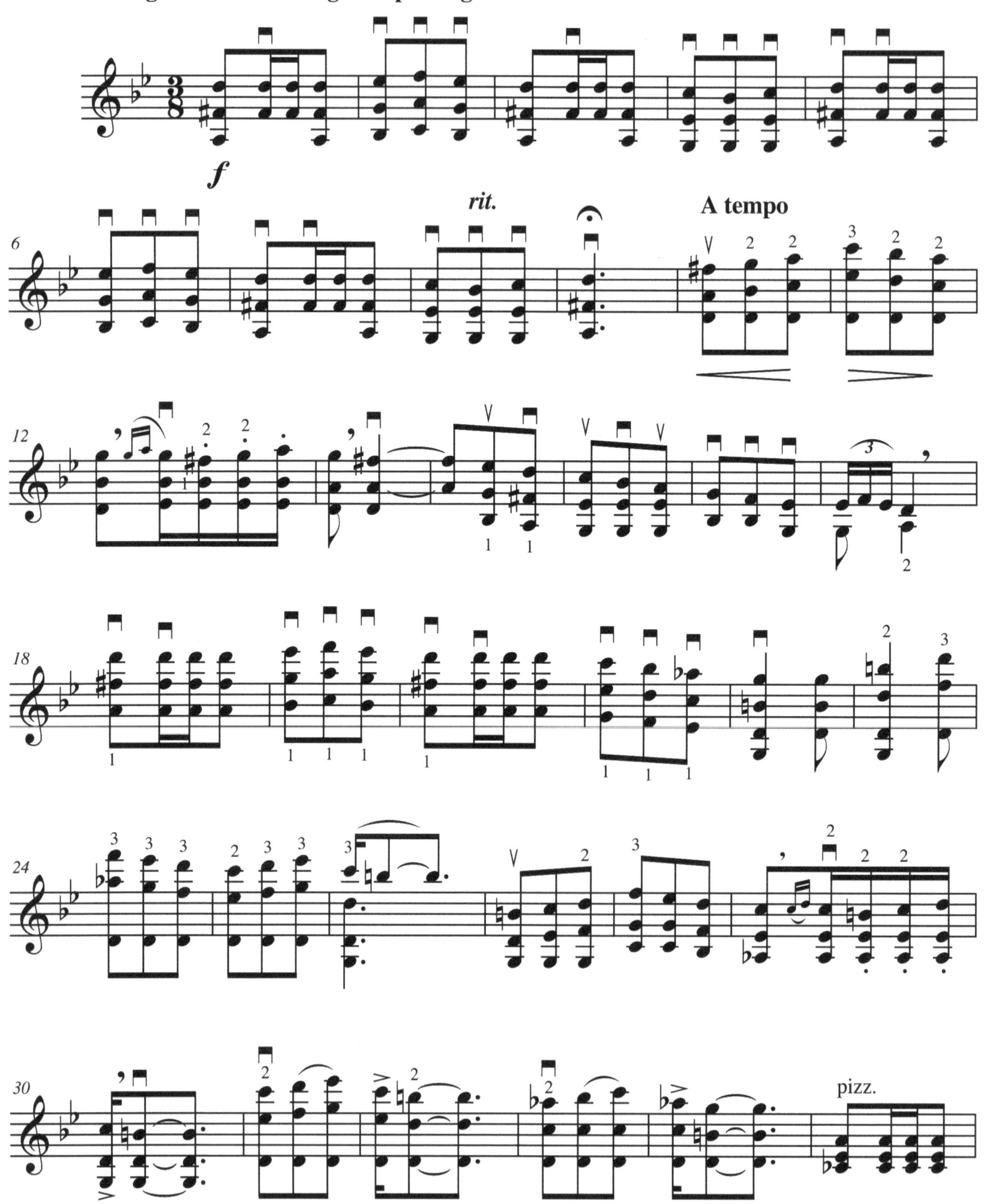

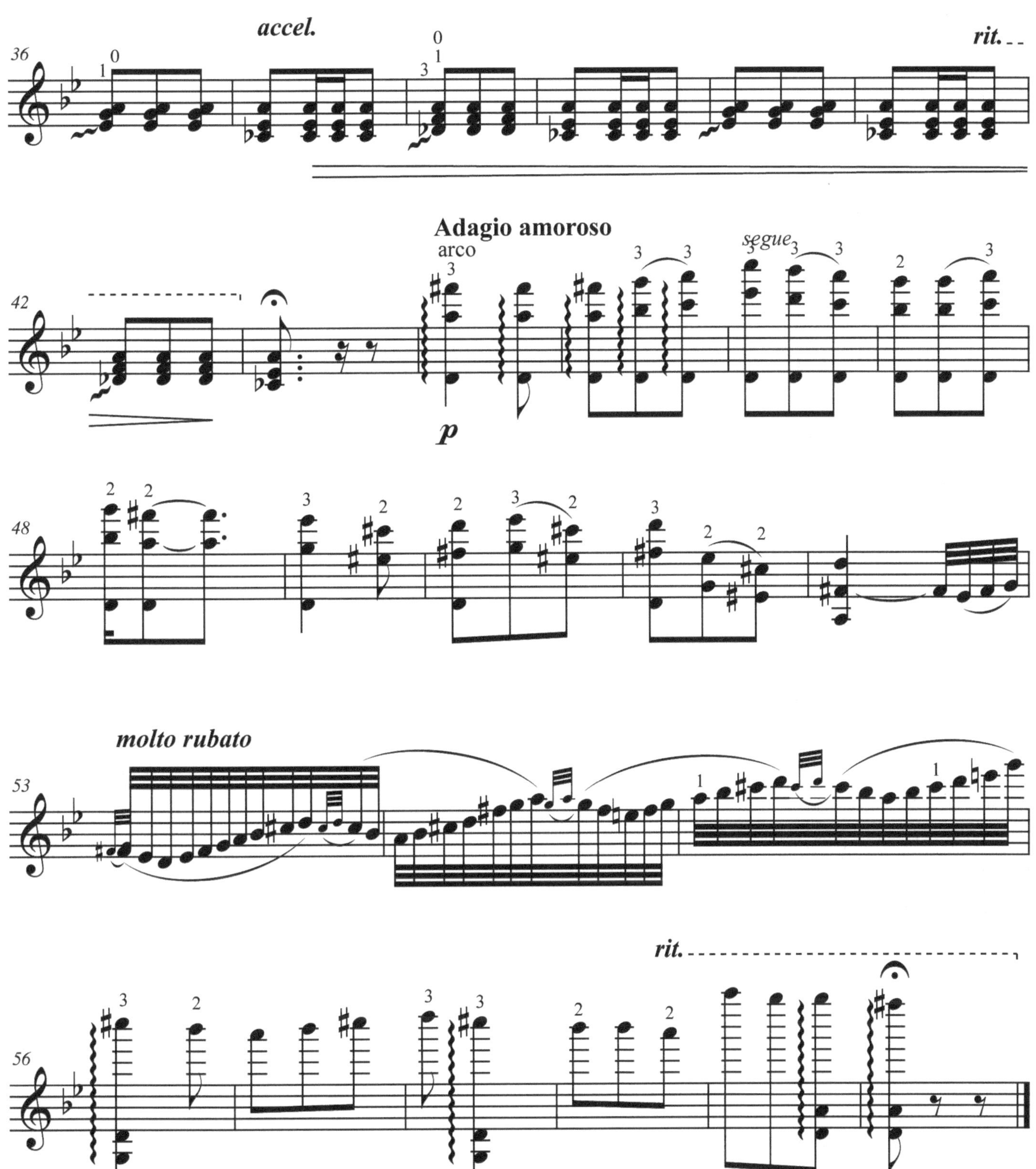
accel.
rit.
Adagio amoroso
arco
segue
p
molto rubato
rit.
pp

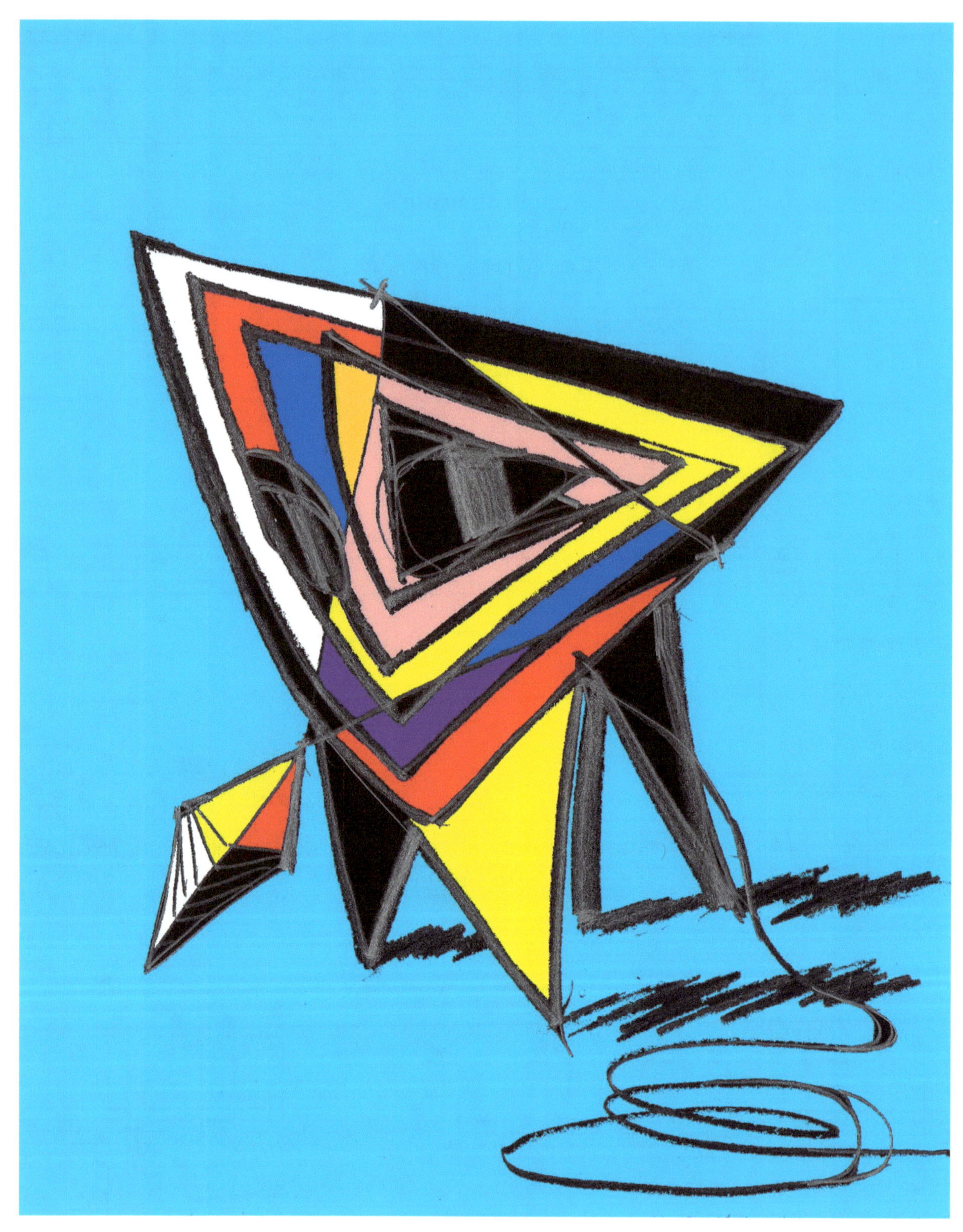

No. 7

"Let's Play"

Day in the Park with Eva and Butterflies

To Rebecca and Eva

VII. Day in the Park with Eva and Butterflies

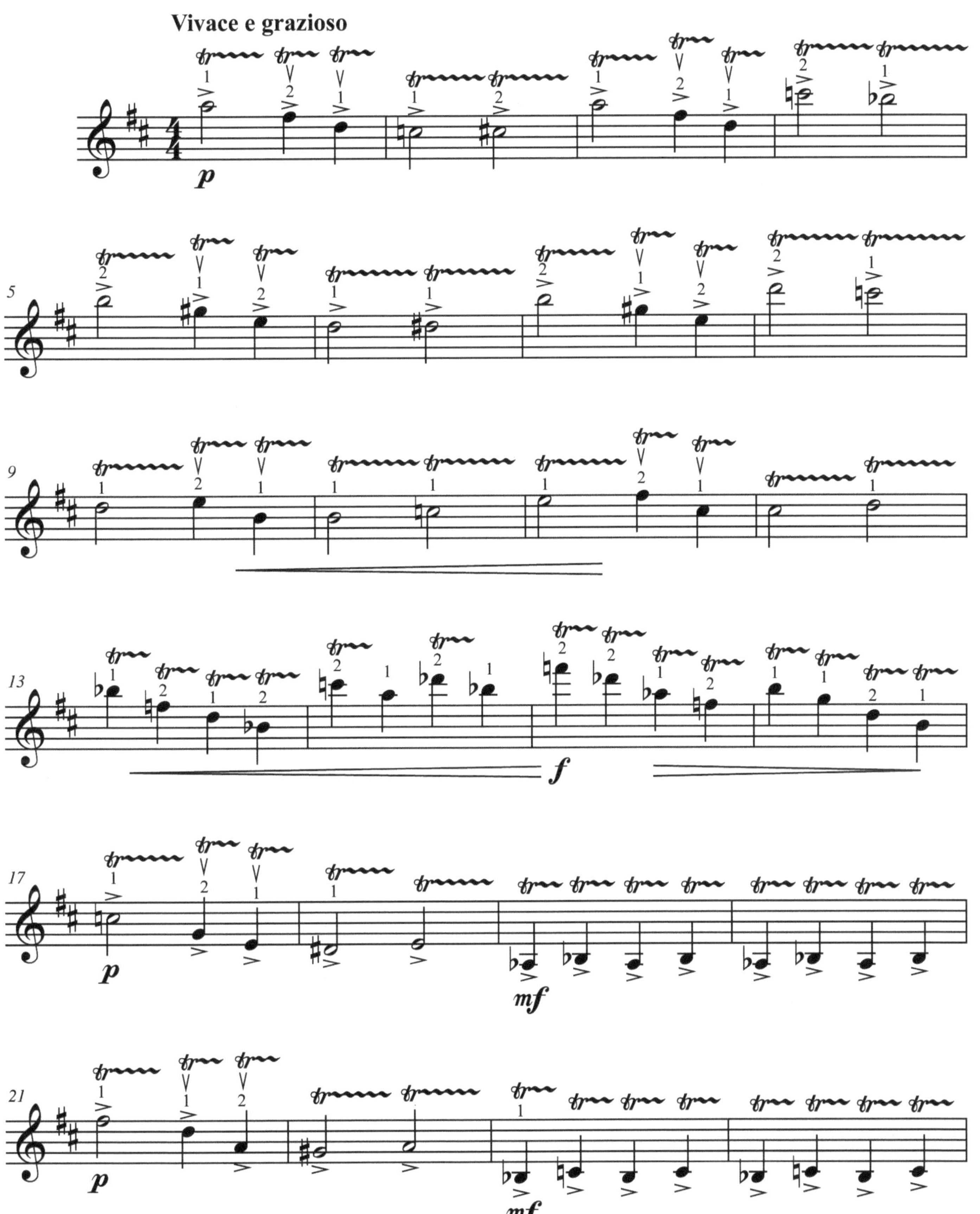

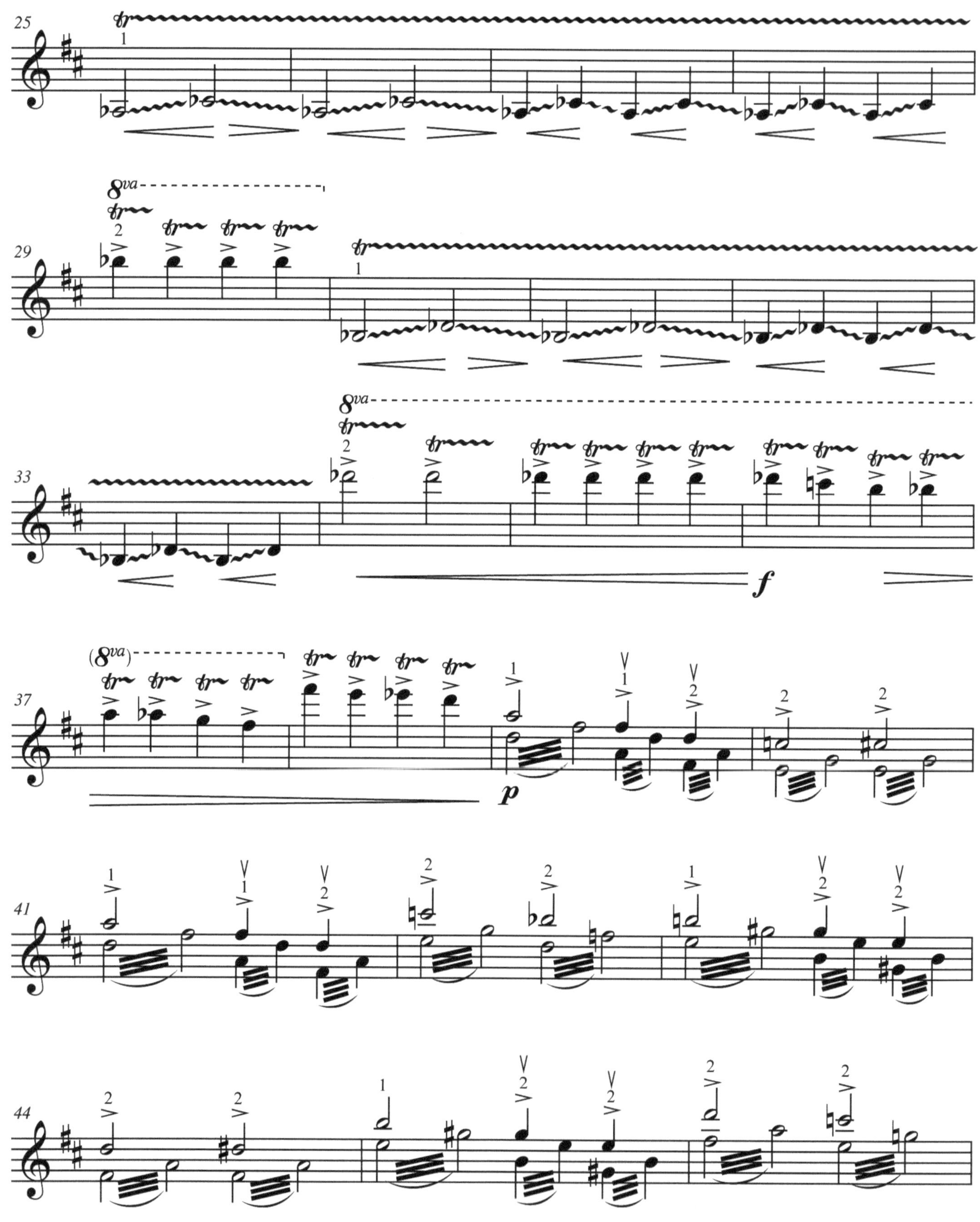
25
29
8va
33
8va
f
37
(8va)
p
41
44

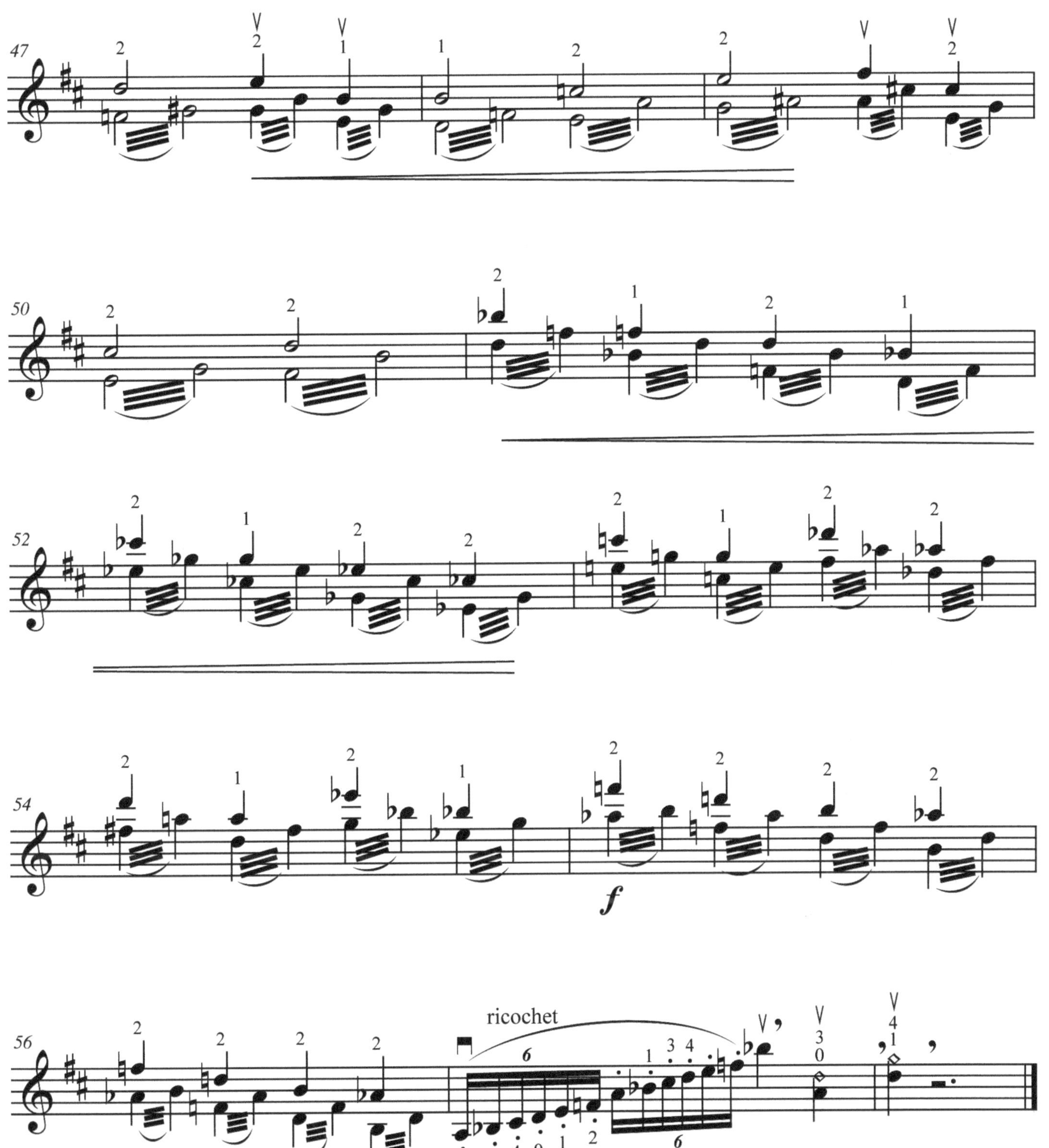
ricochet
f
p

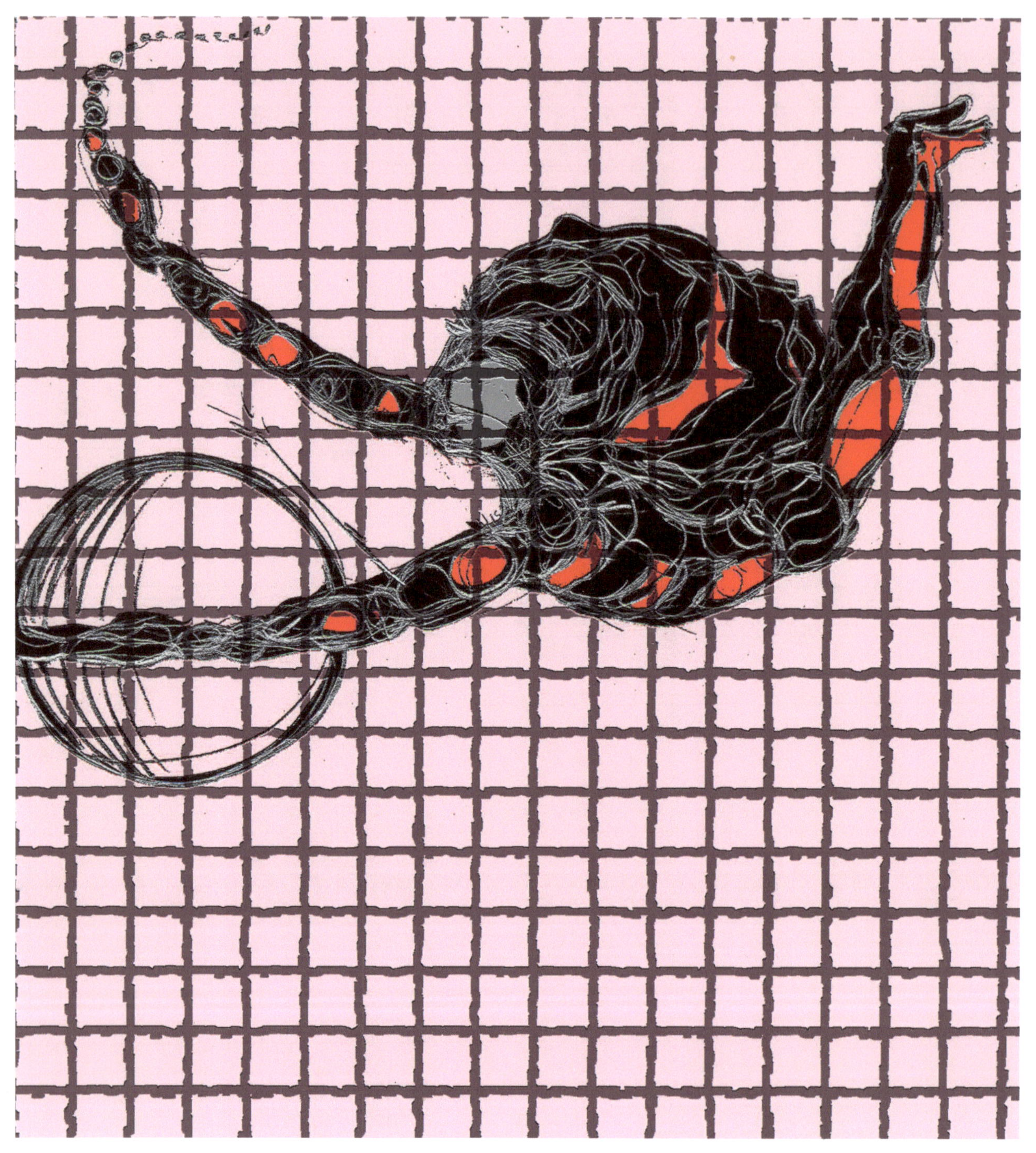

No. 8
Taming the Ball

To Tiffany Modell

VIII. Taming the Ball

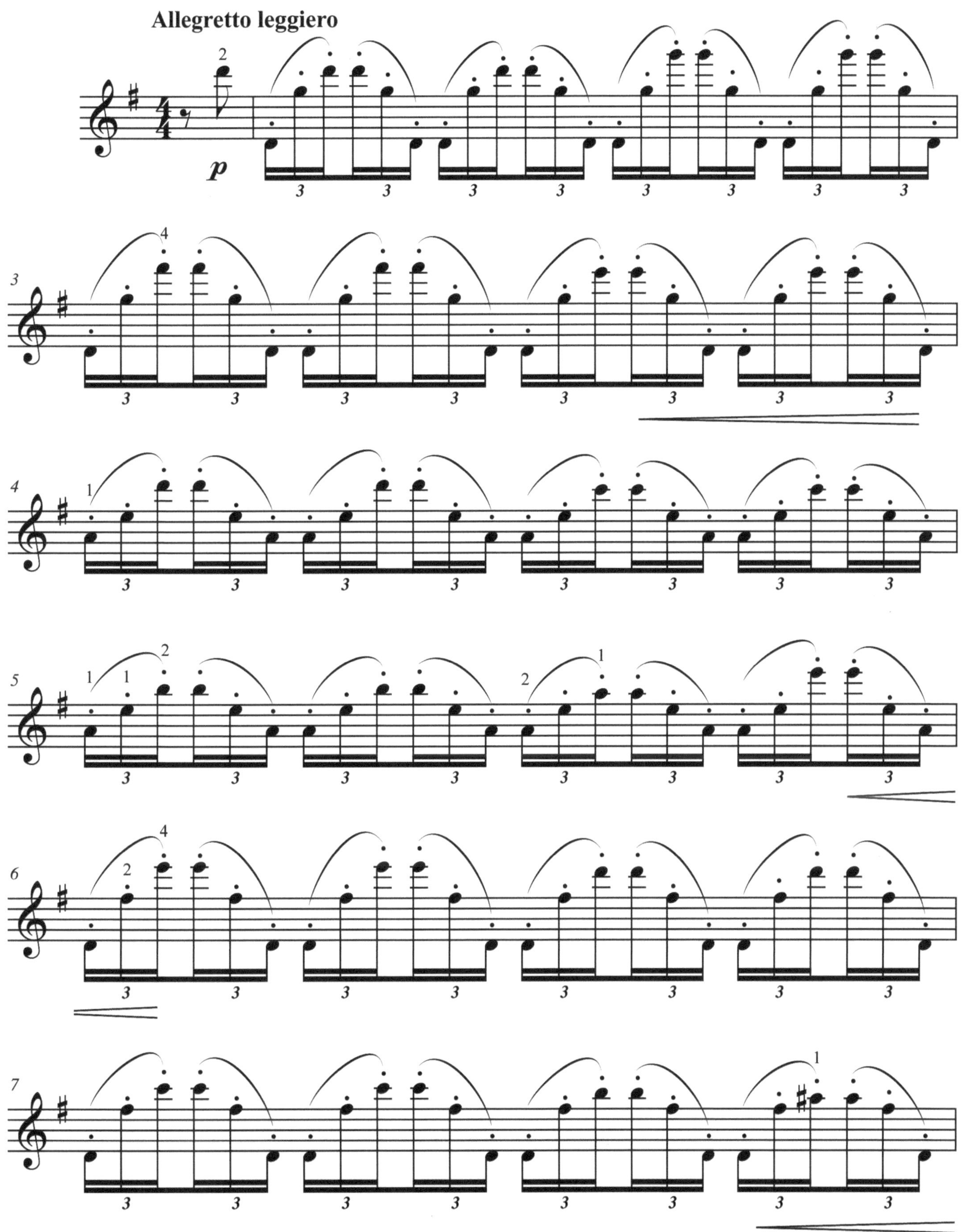

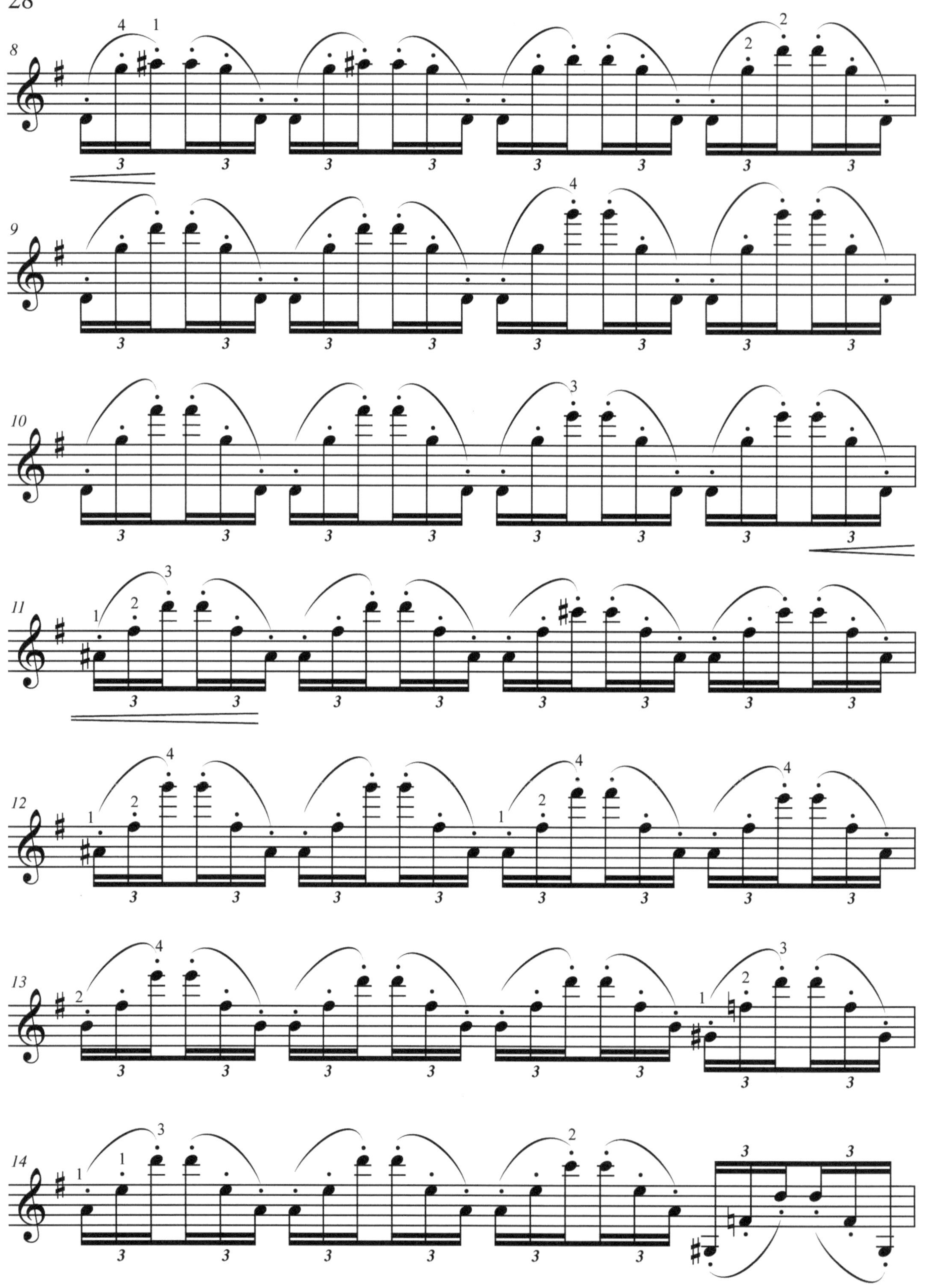

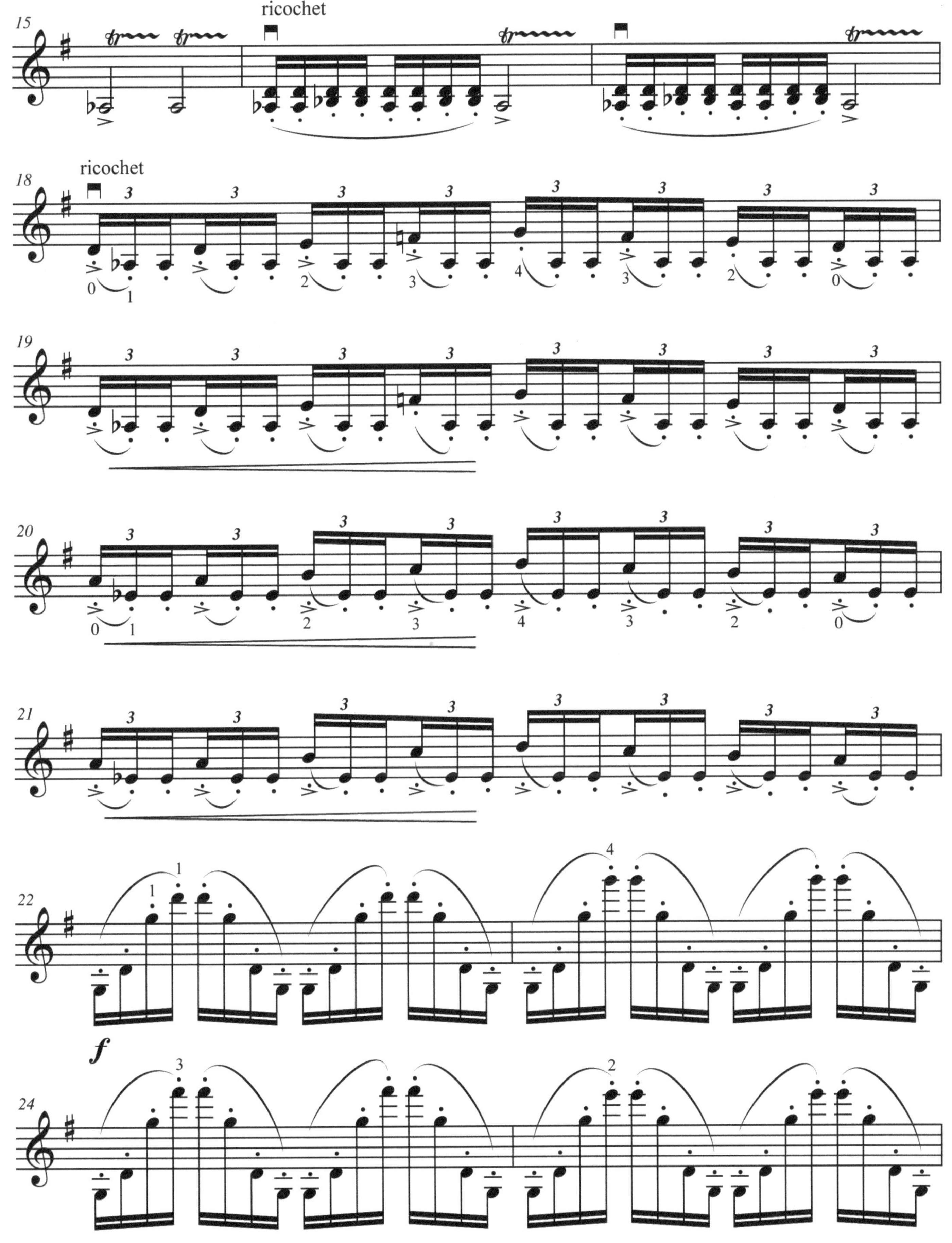
ricochet
ricochet
f

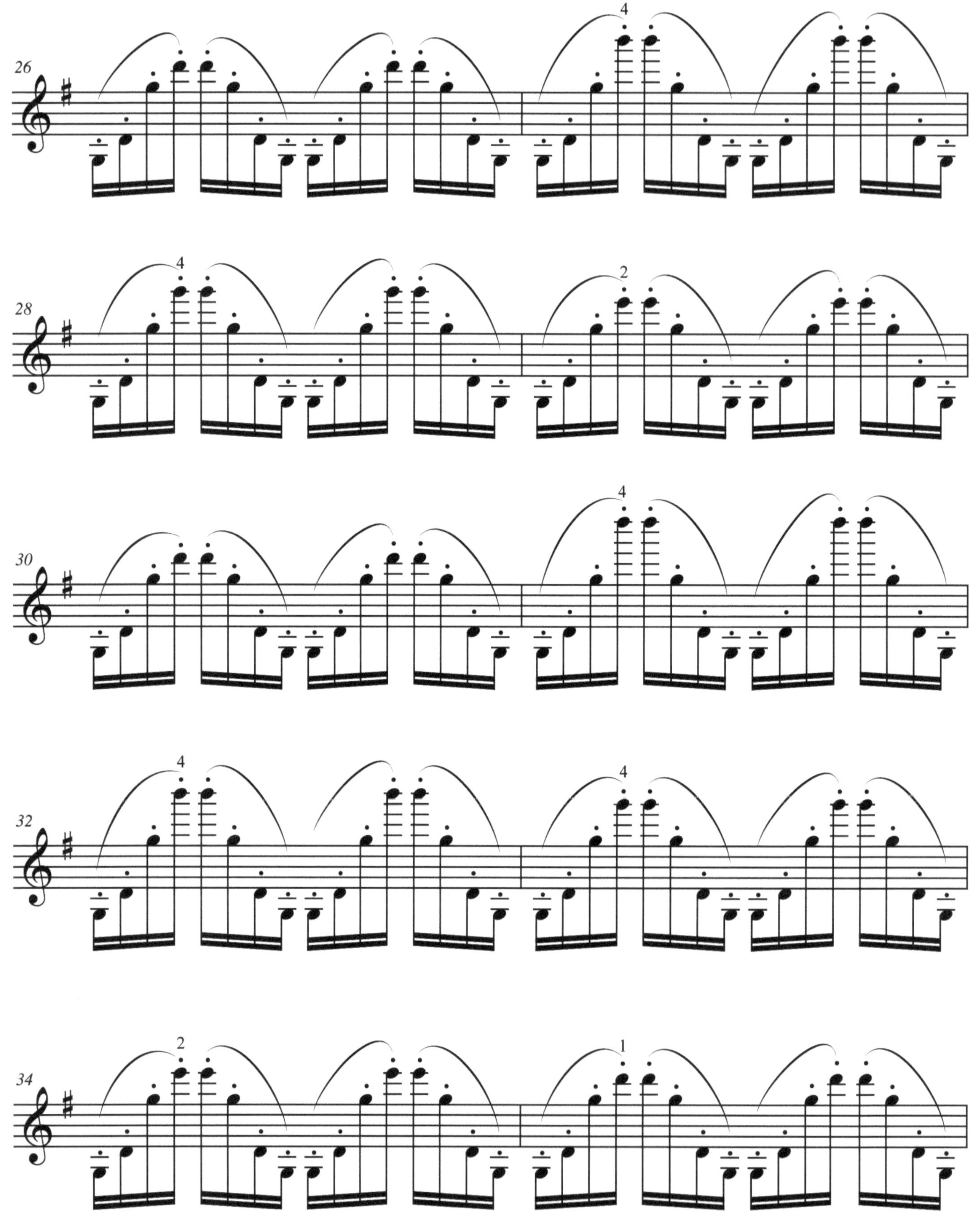
26
28
30
32
34

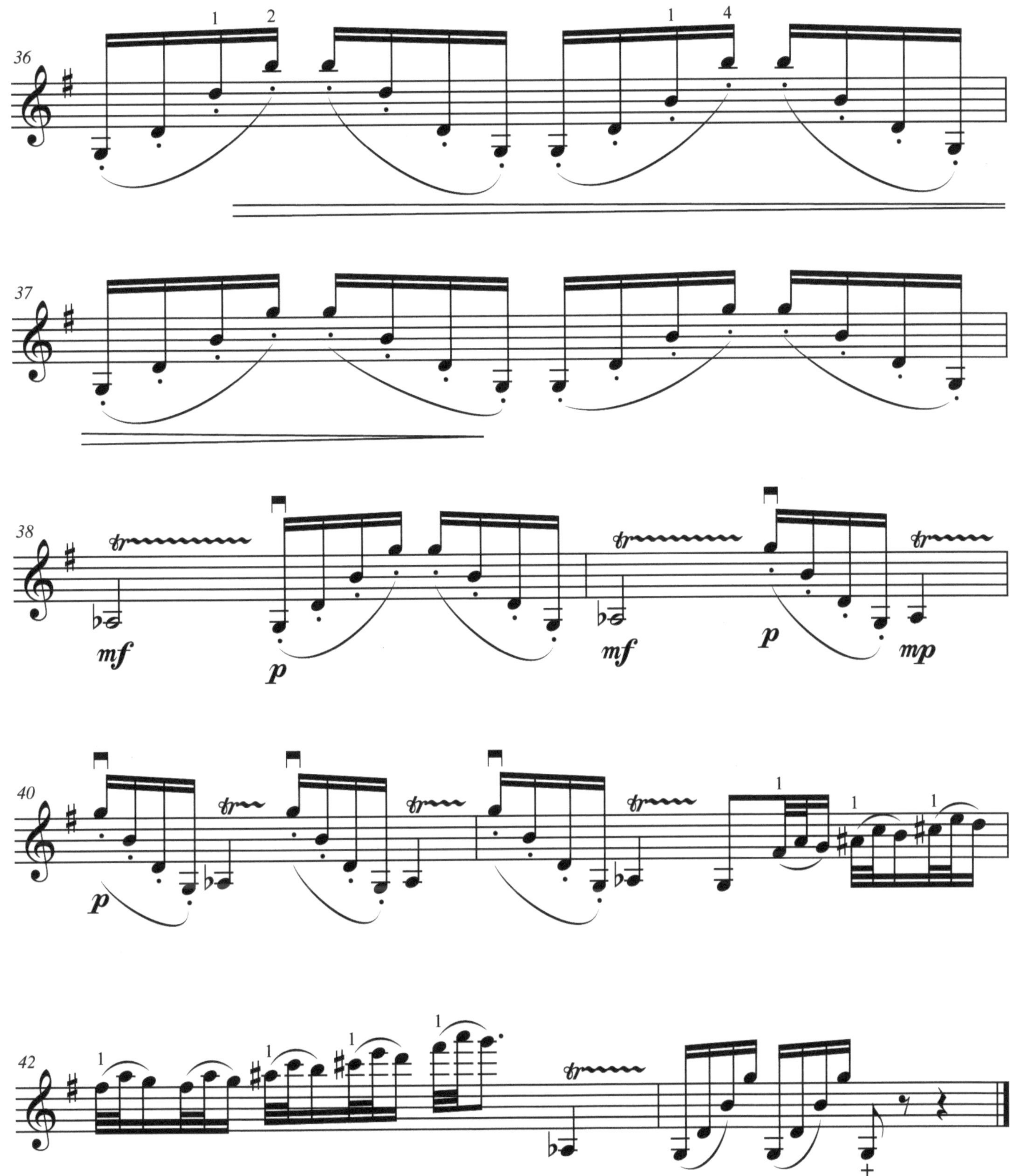
36
1
2
1
4
37
38
mf
p
mf
p
mp
40
p
1
1
1
42
1
1
1
1

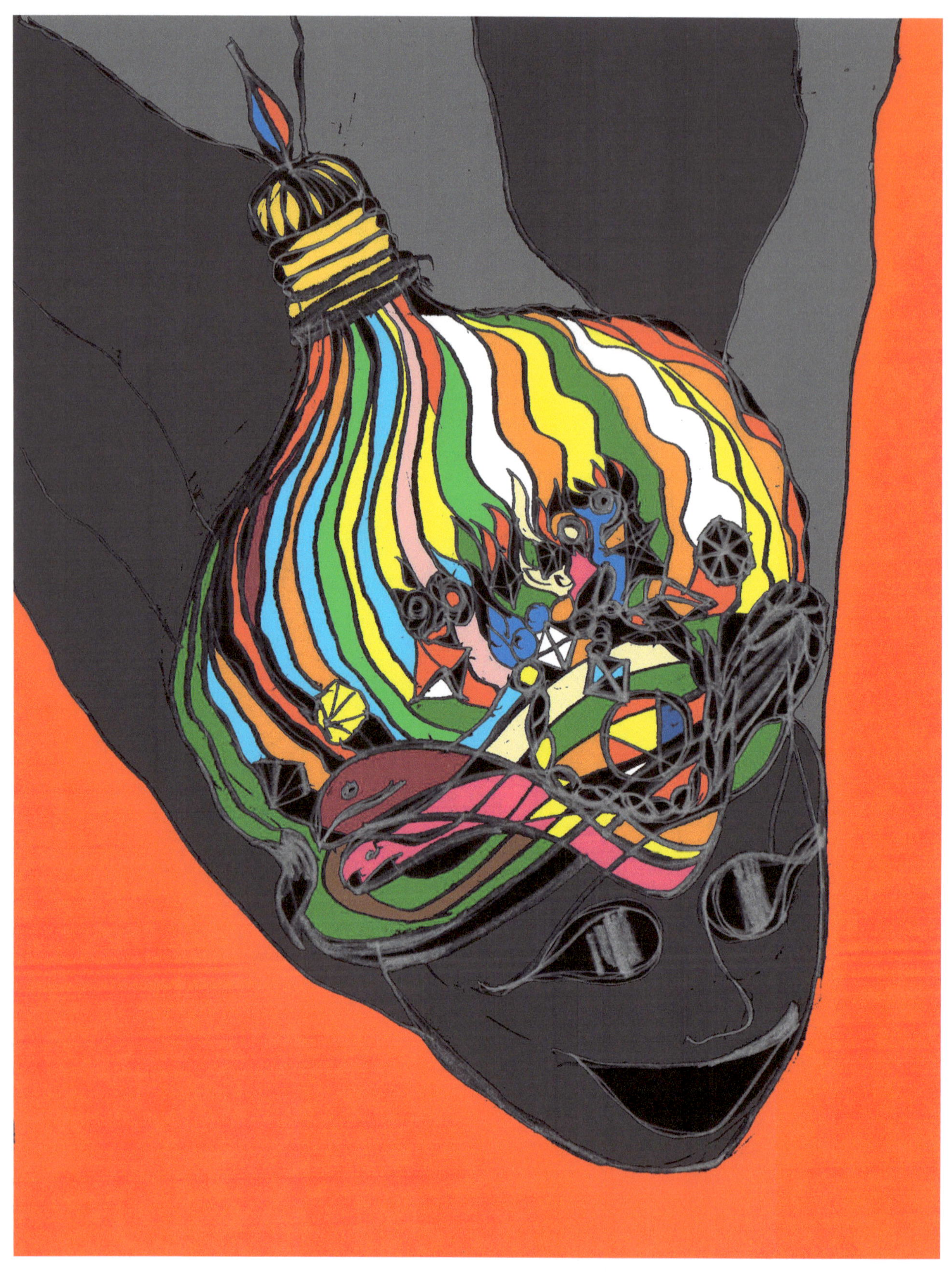

No. 9
Cell Phone Polka

To Sasha

IX. Cell Phone Polka

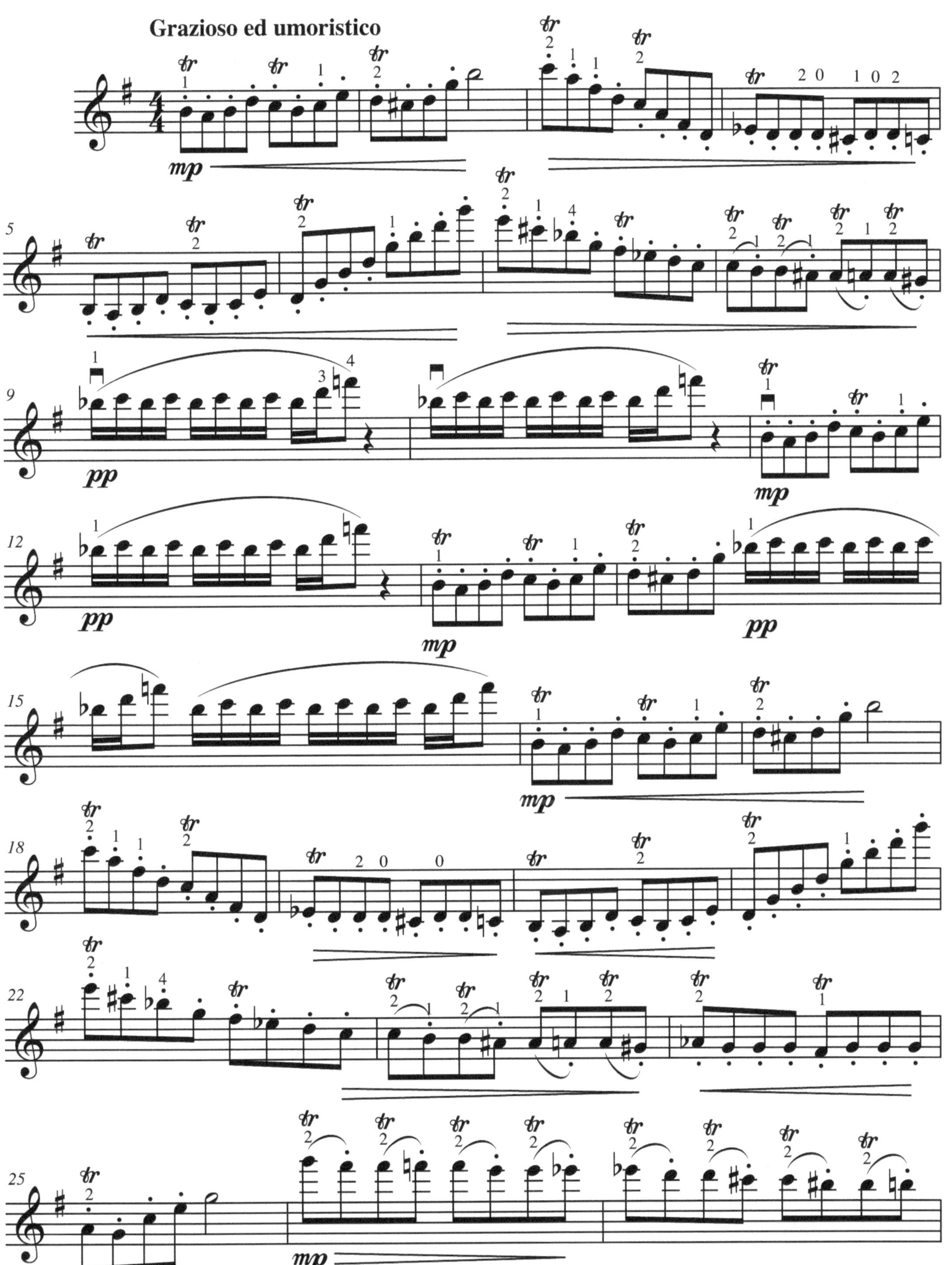

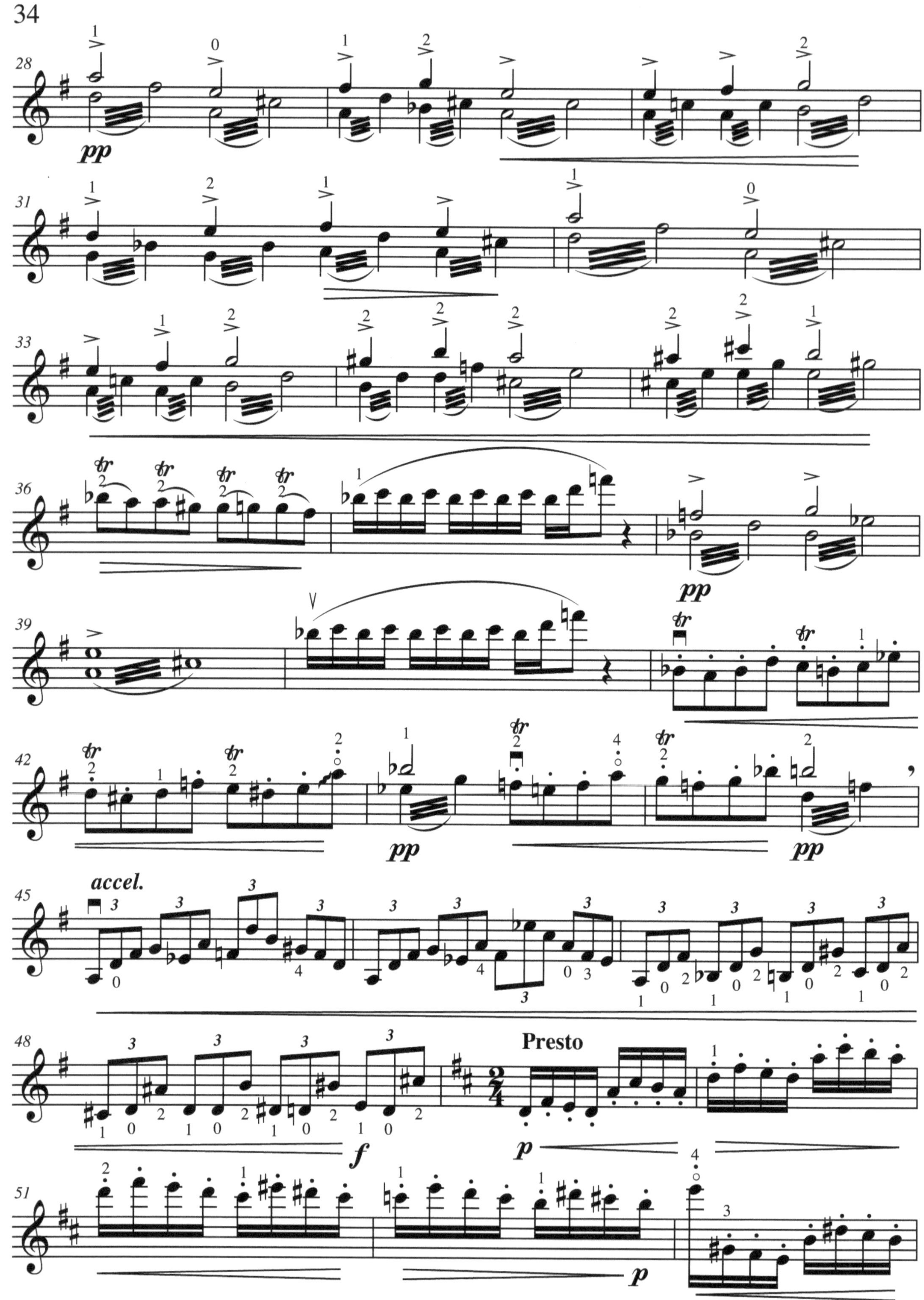
pp
accel.
Presto
f
p

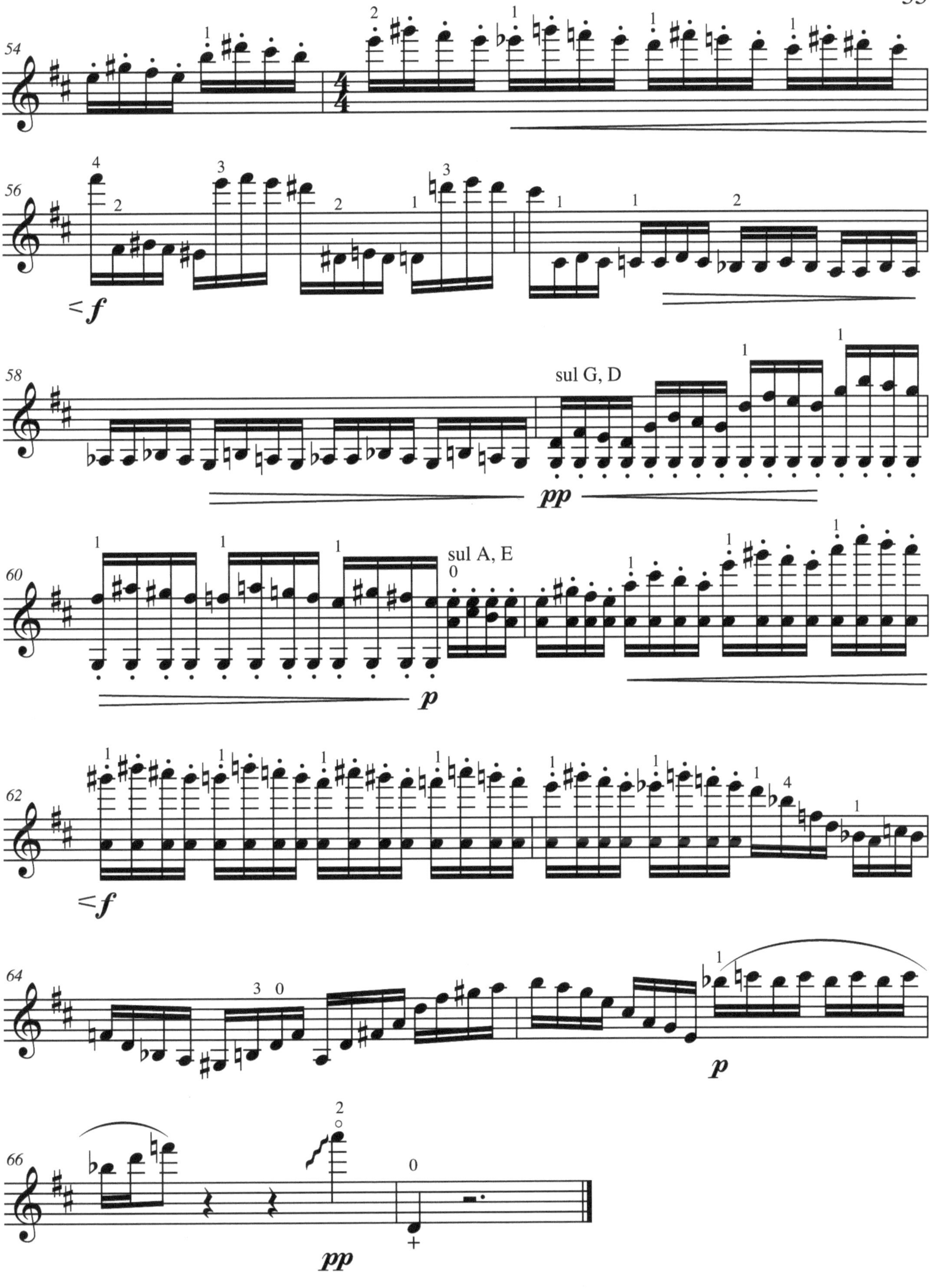

54

56

58

sul G, D

60

sul A, E

62

64

66

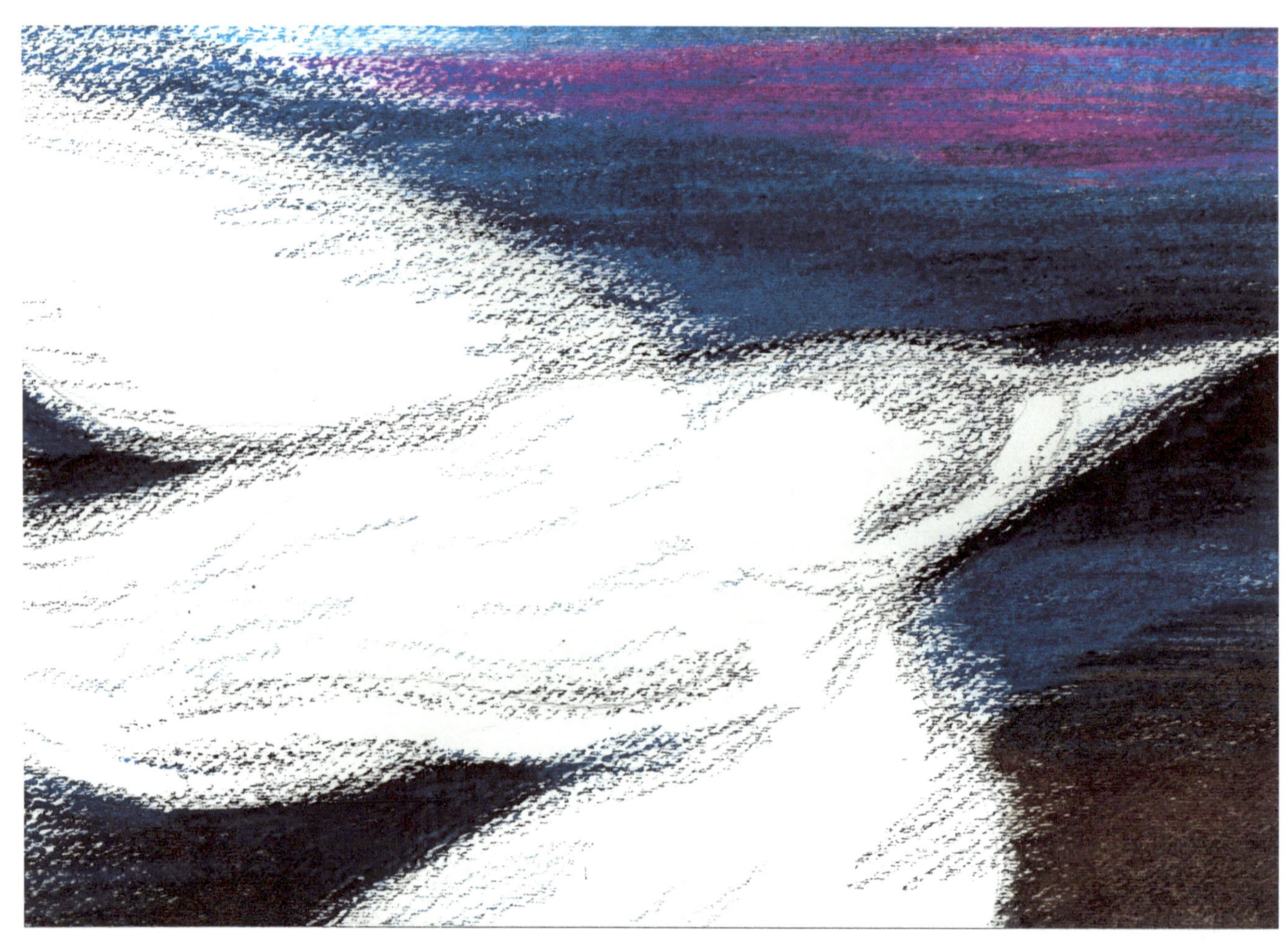

No. 10
Midnight Flight

To Masaoki Inoue

X. Midnight Flight

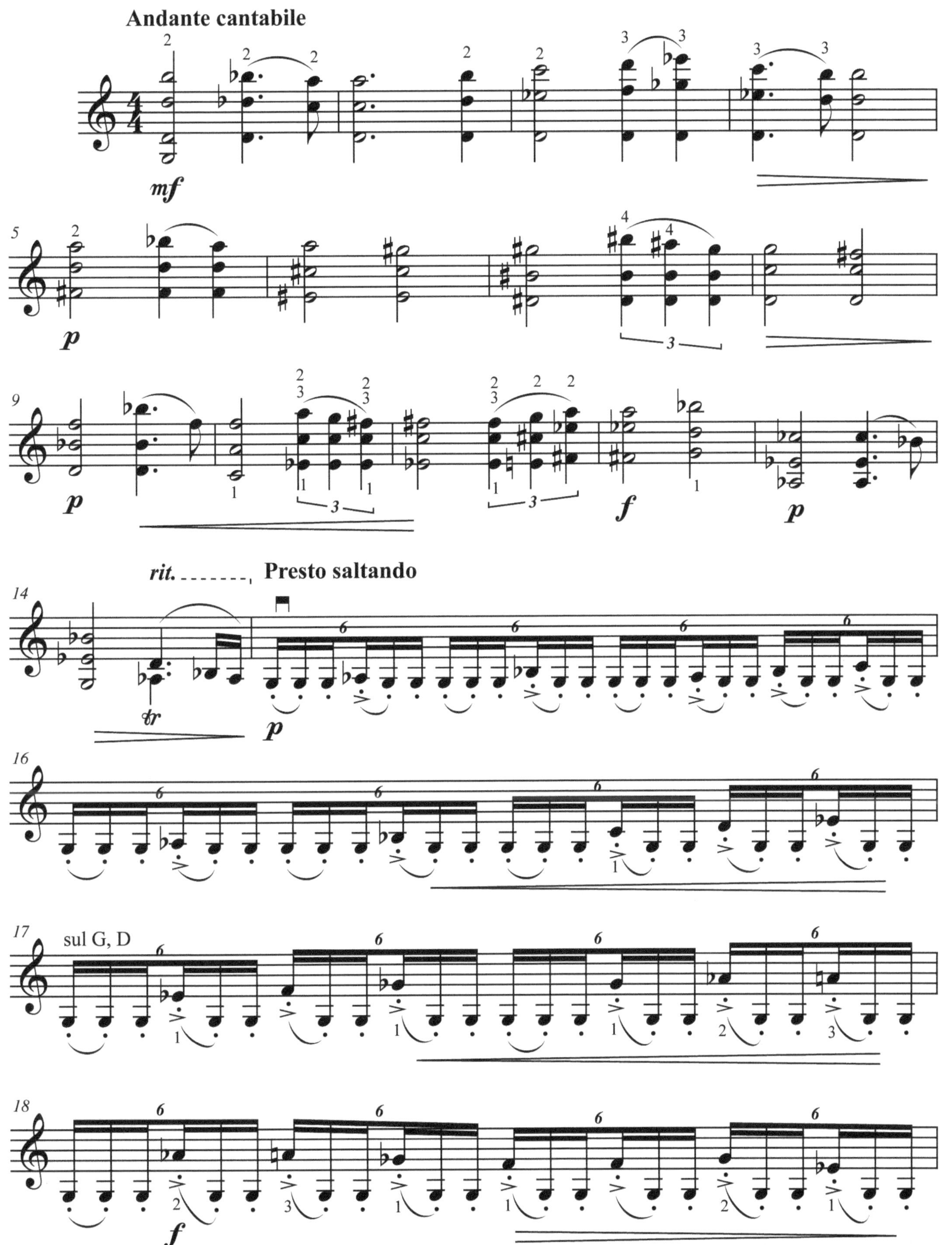

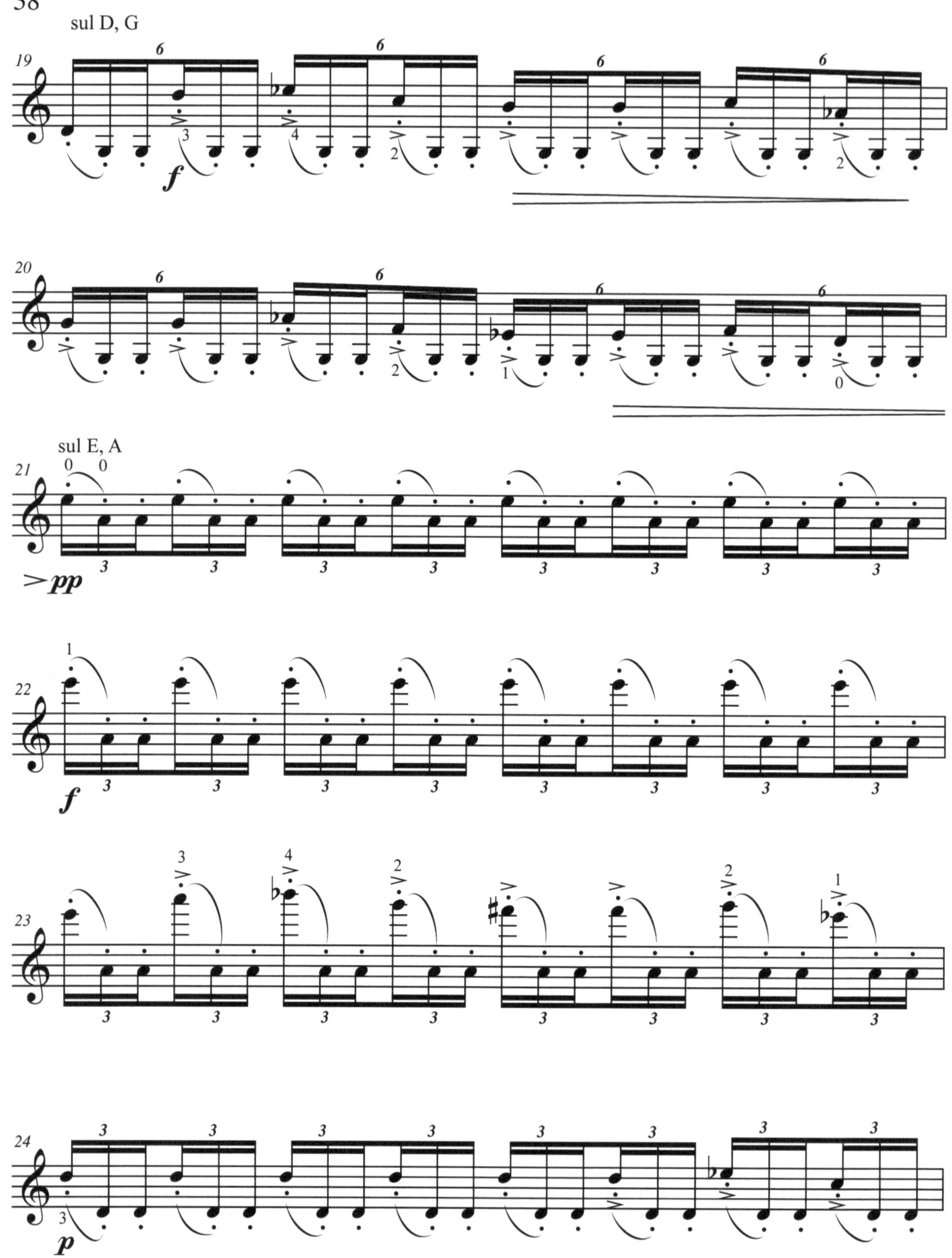
sul D, G
f
sul E, A
pp
f
p

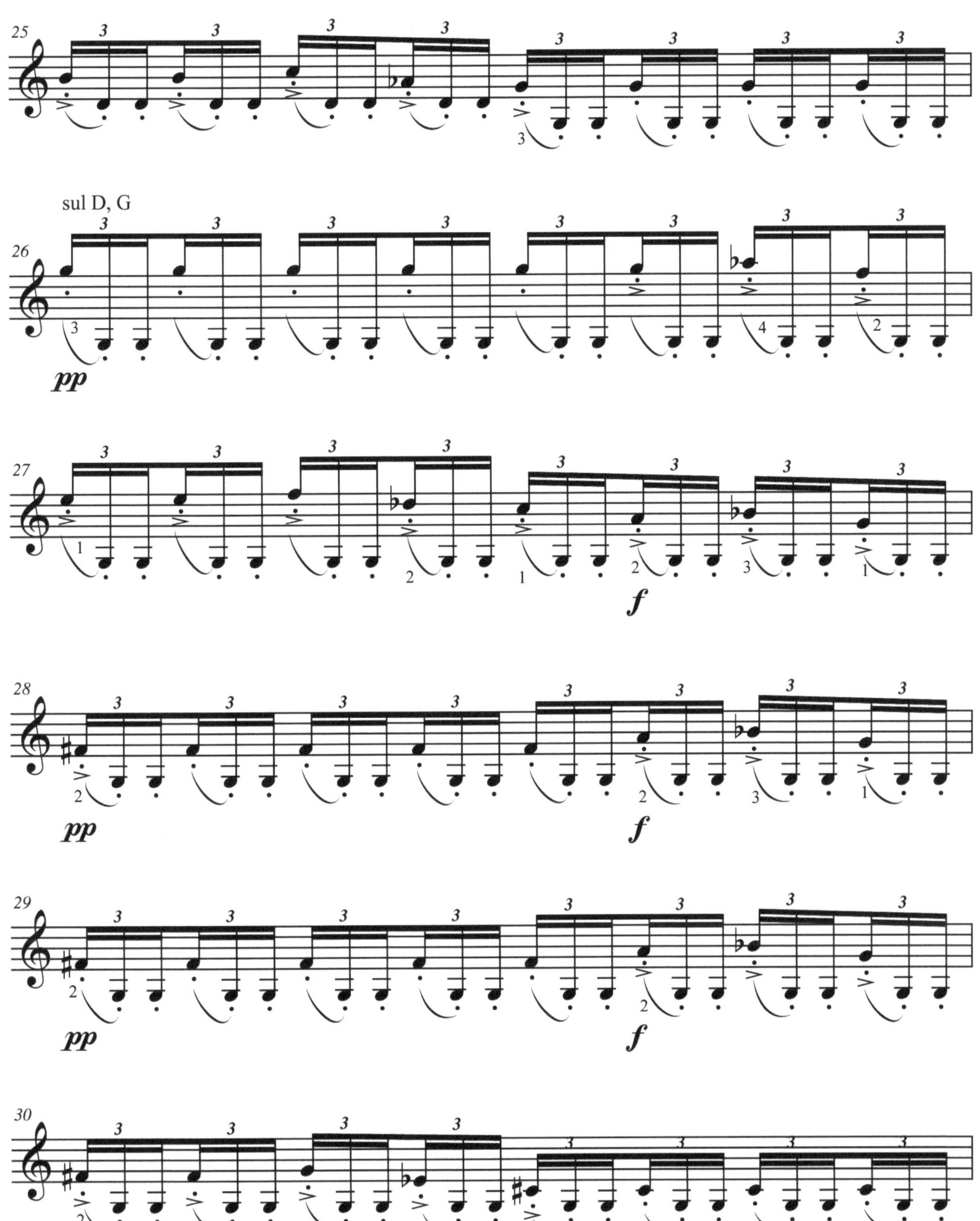
sul D, G
pp
f
pp
f
pp
f

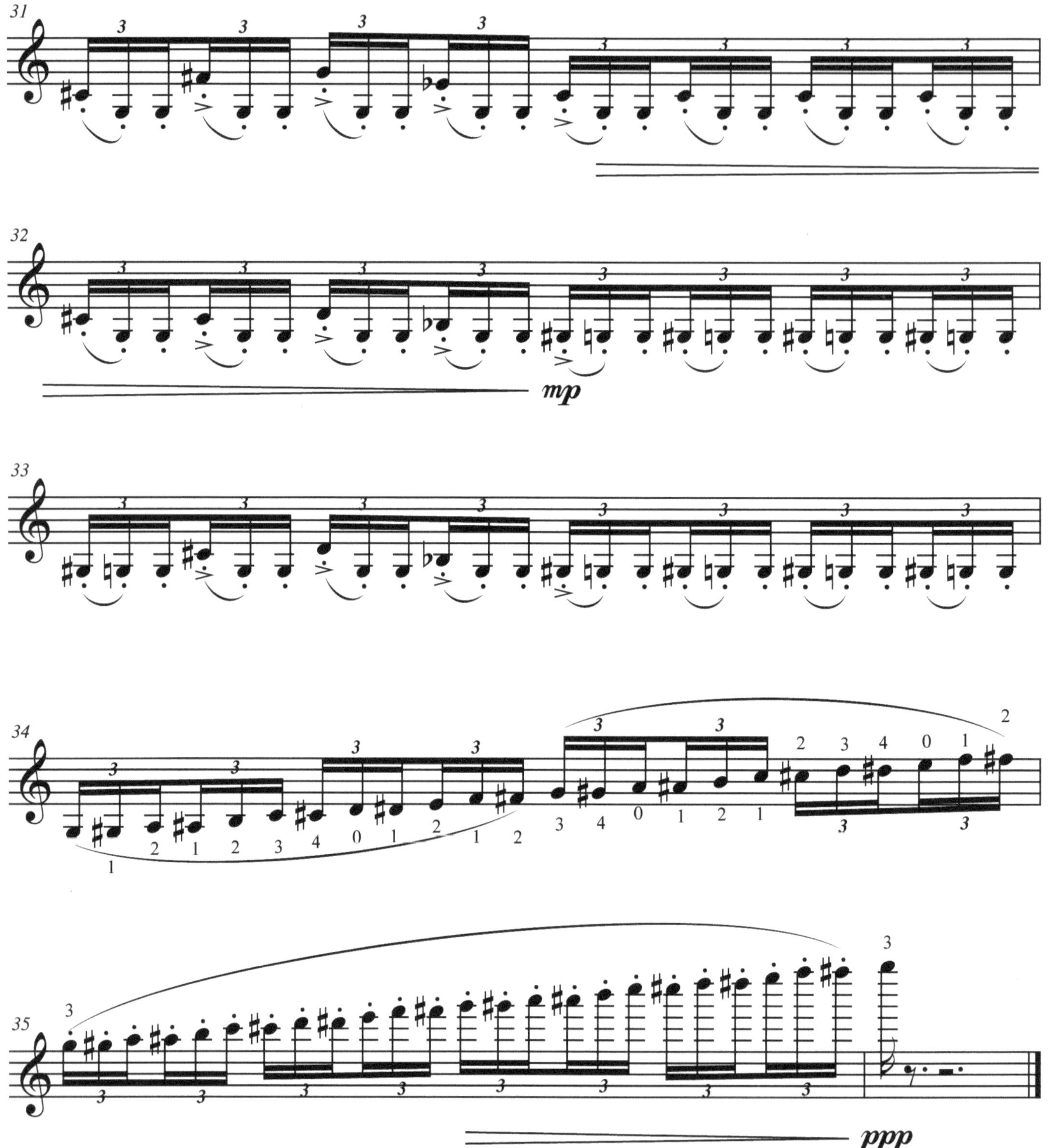

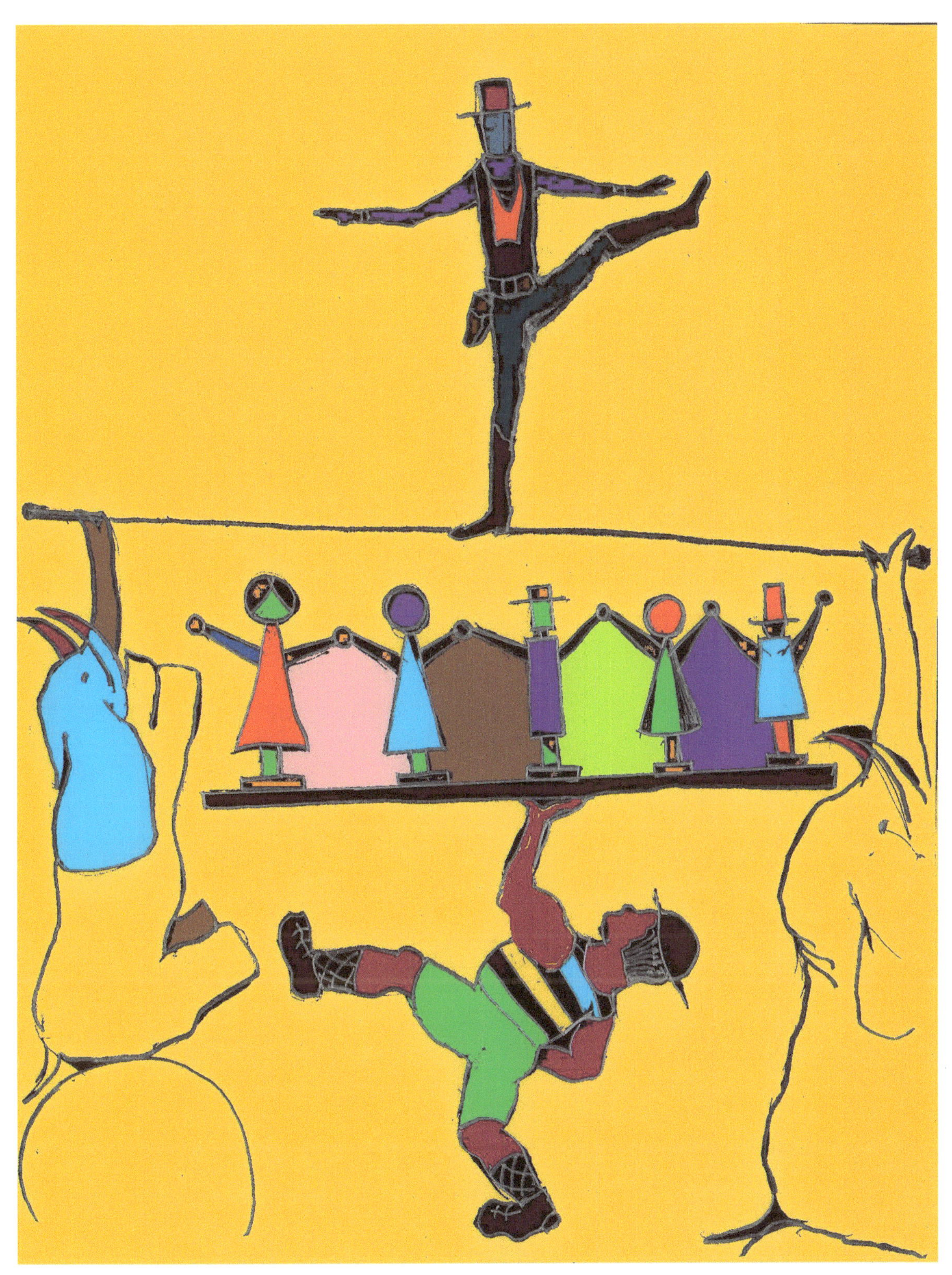

No. 11
You Can Do It!

To Paul Lindenauer

XI. You Can Do It!

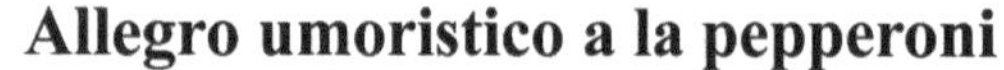

pizz.

Andante Spagnolo

segue

rit. ---------------------------------- A tempo

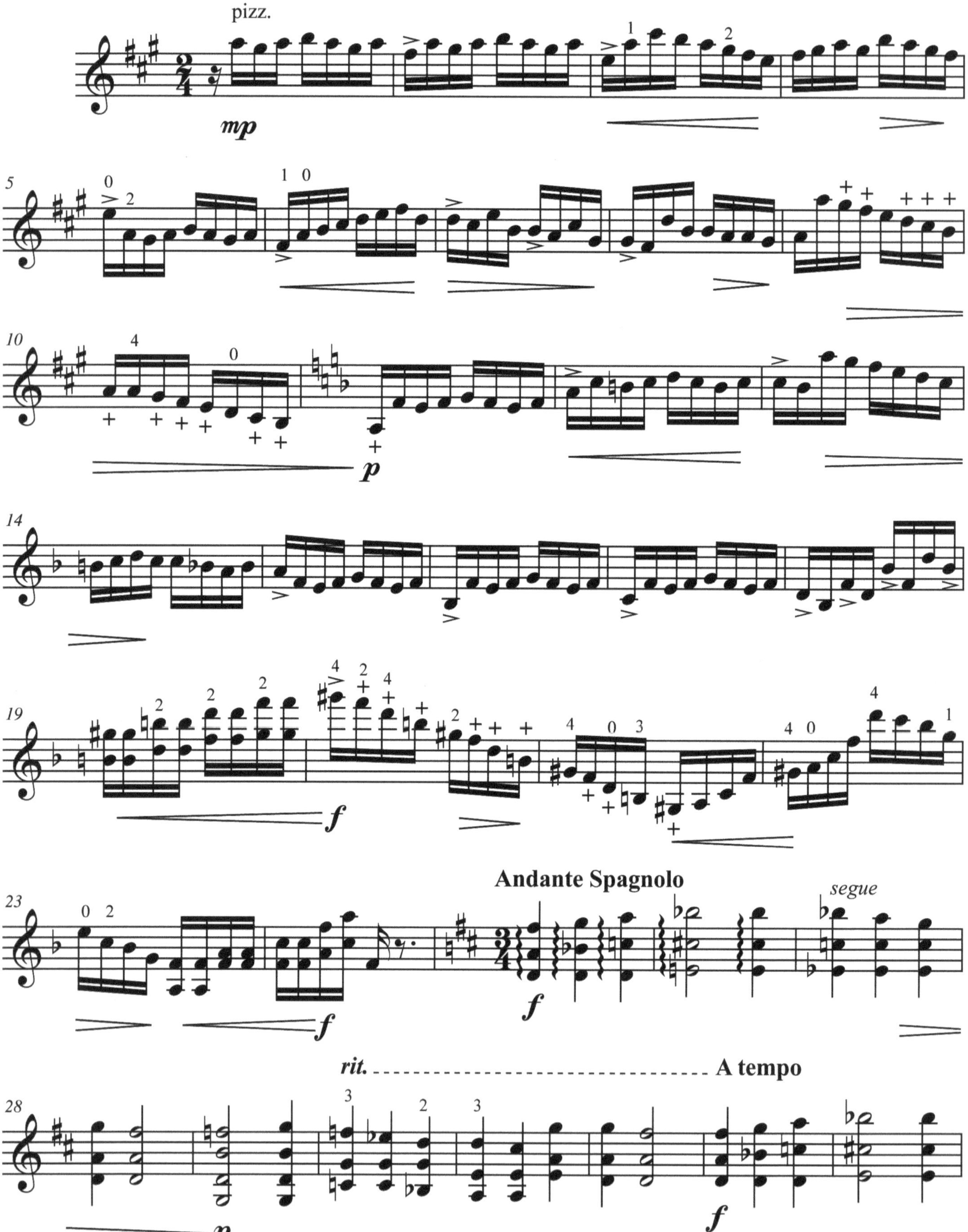

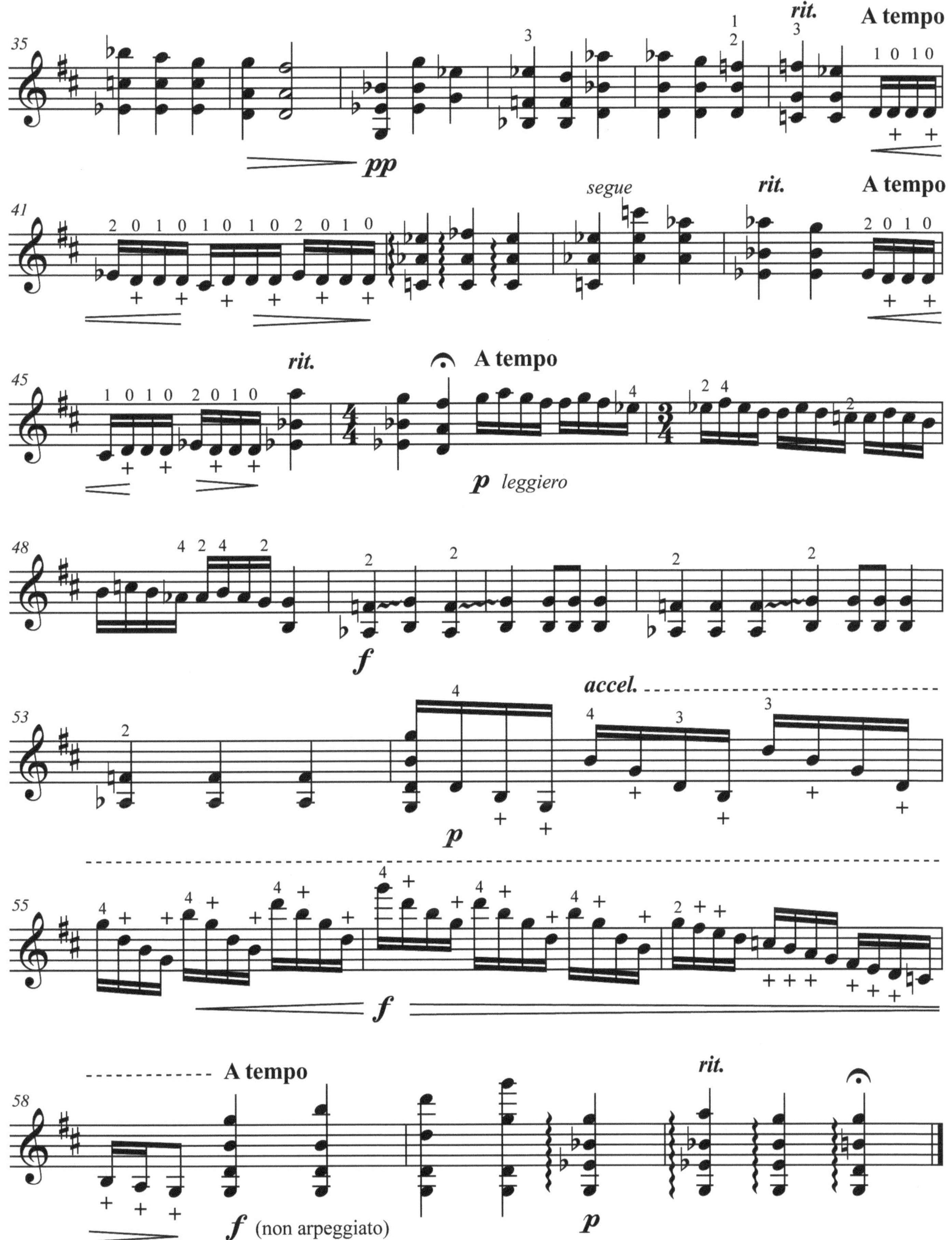
35
rit.
A tempo
pp
41
segue
rit.
A tempo
45
rit.
A tempo
p leggiero
48
f
53
accel.
p
55
f
58
A tempo
rit.
f (non arpeggiato)
p

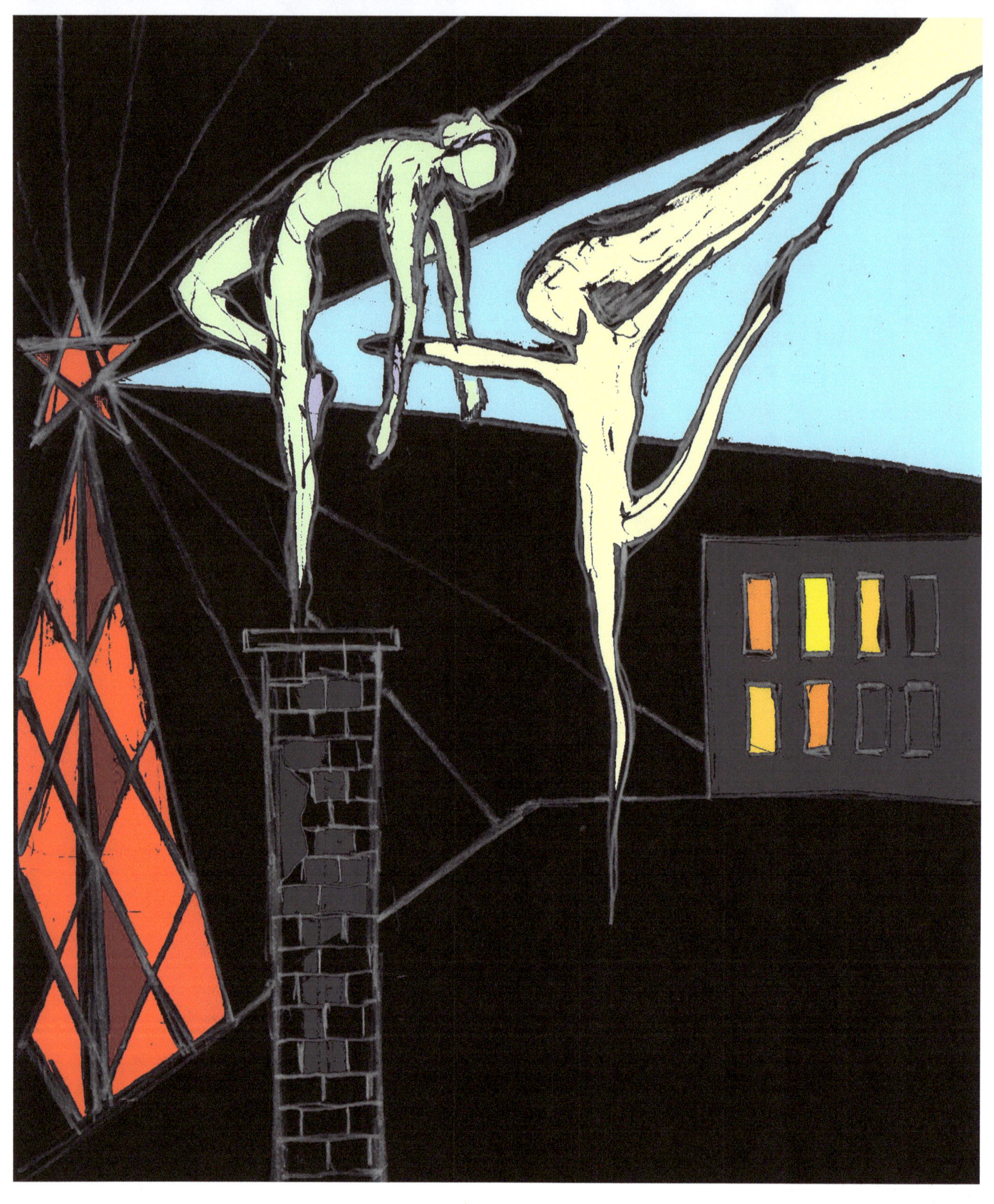

No. 12
Midnight Serenade in the Style
of K.Szymanowski

To Pasha

XII. Midnight Serenade in the Style of K. Szymanowski

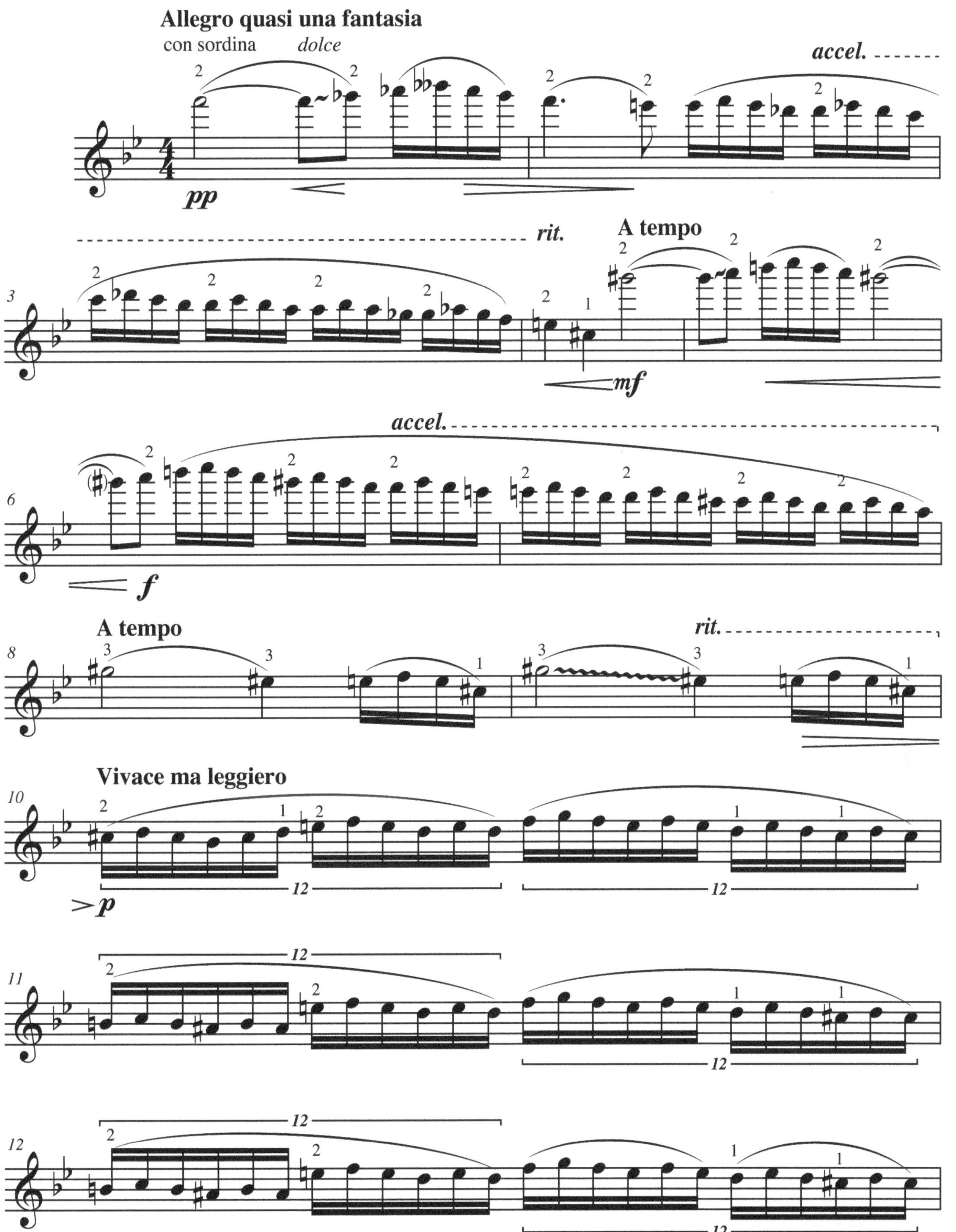

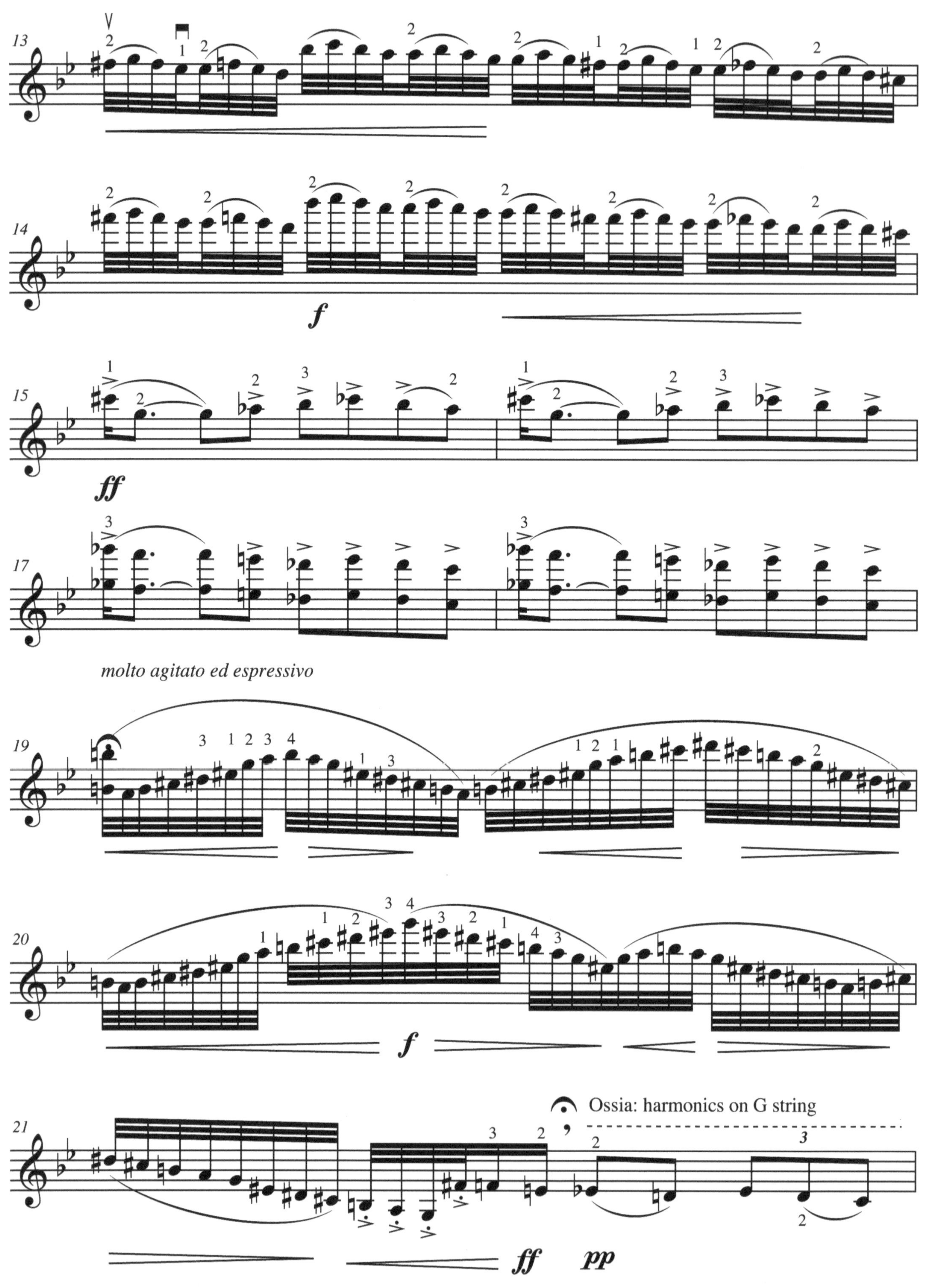
molto agitato ed espressivo
Ossia: harmonics on G string

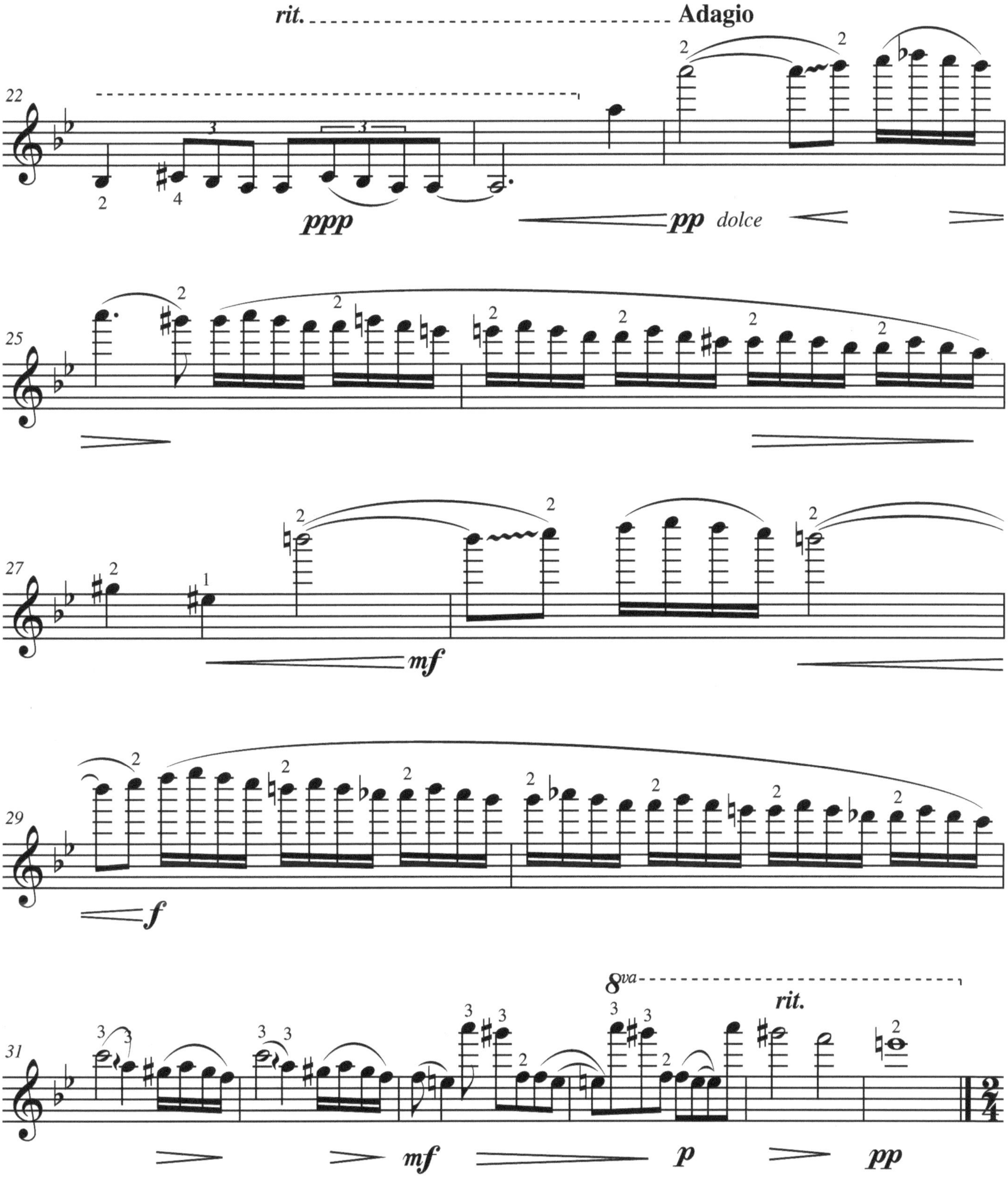

rit. Adagio

22 *ppp* *pp* *dolce*

25

27 *mf*

29 *f*

31 8va *rit.* *mf* *p* *pp*

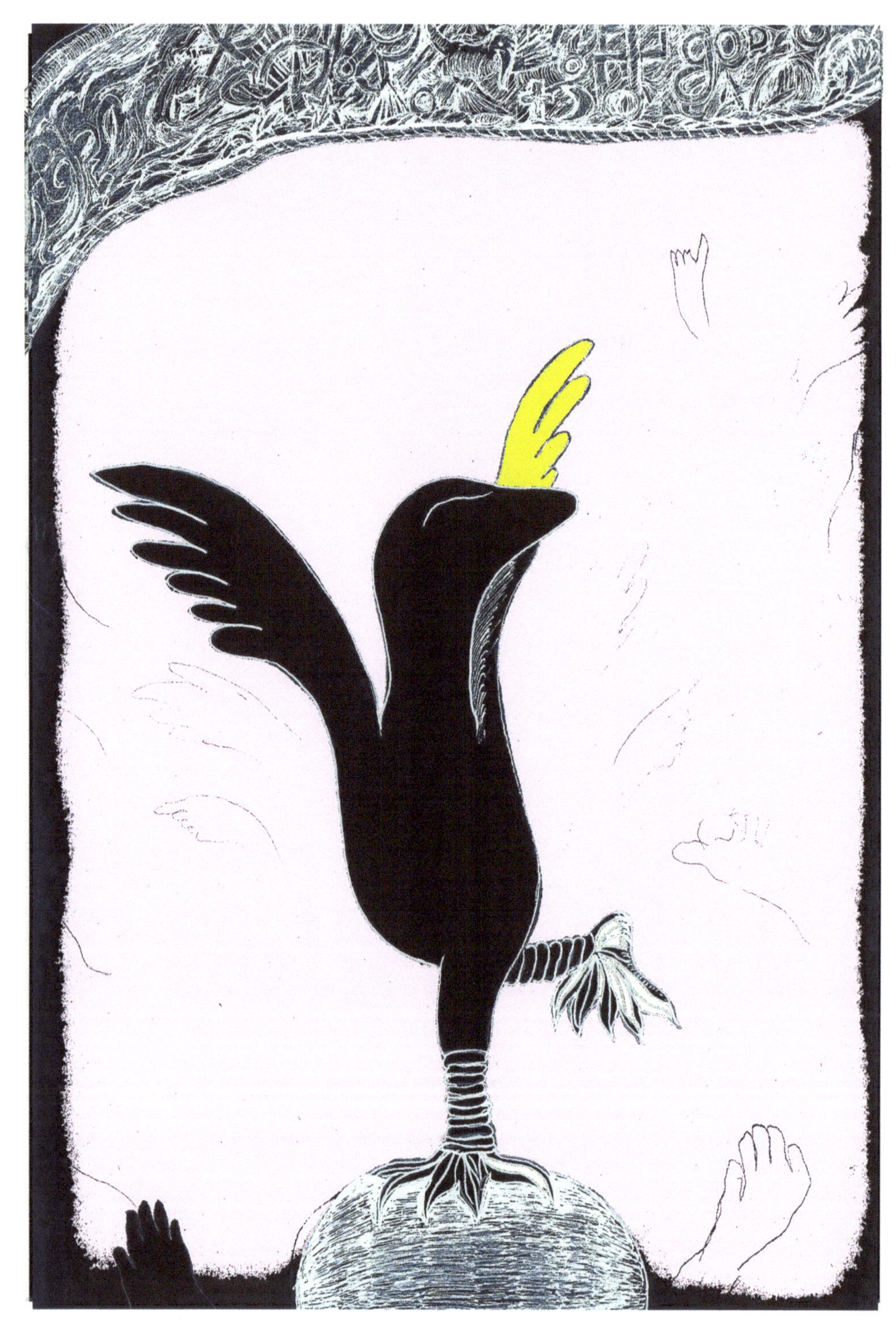

No. 13
Youth and Incredible Lightness of Being in Taos

XIII. Youth and Incredible Lightness of Being in Taos

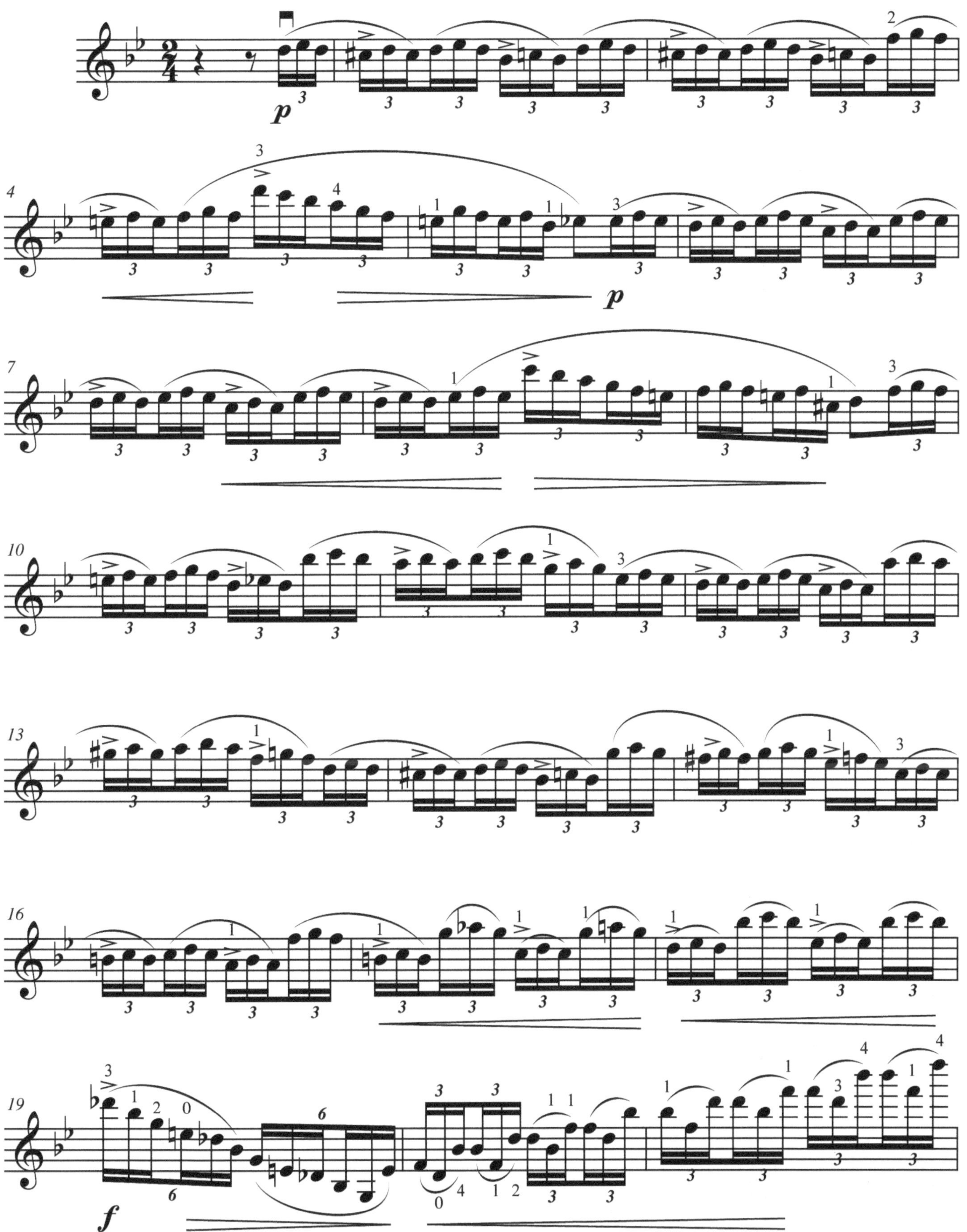

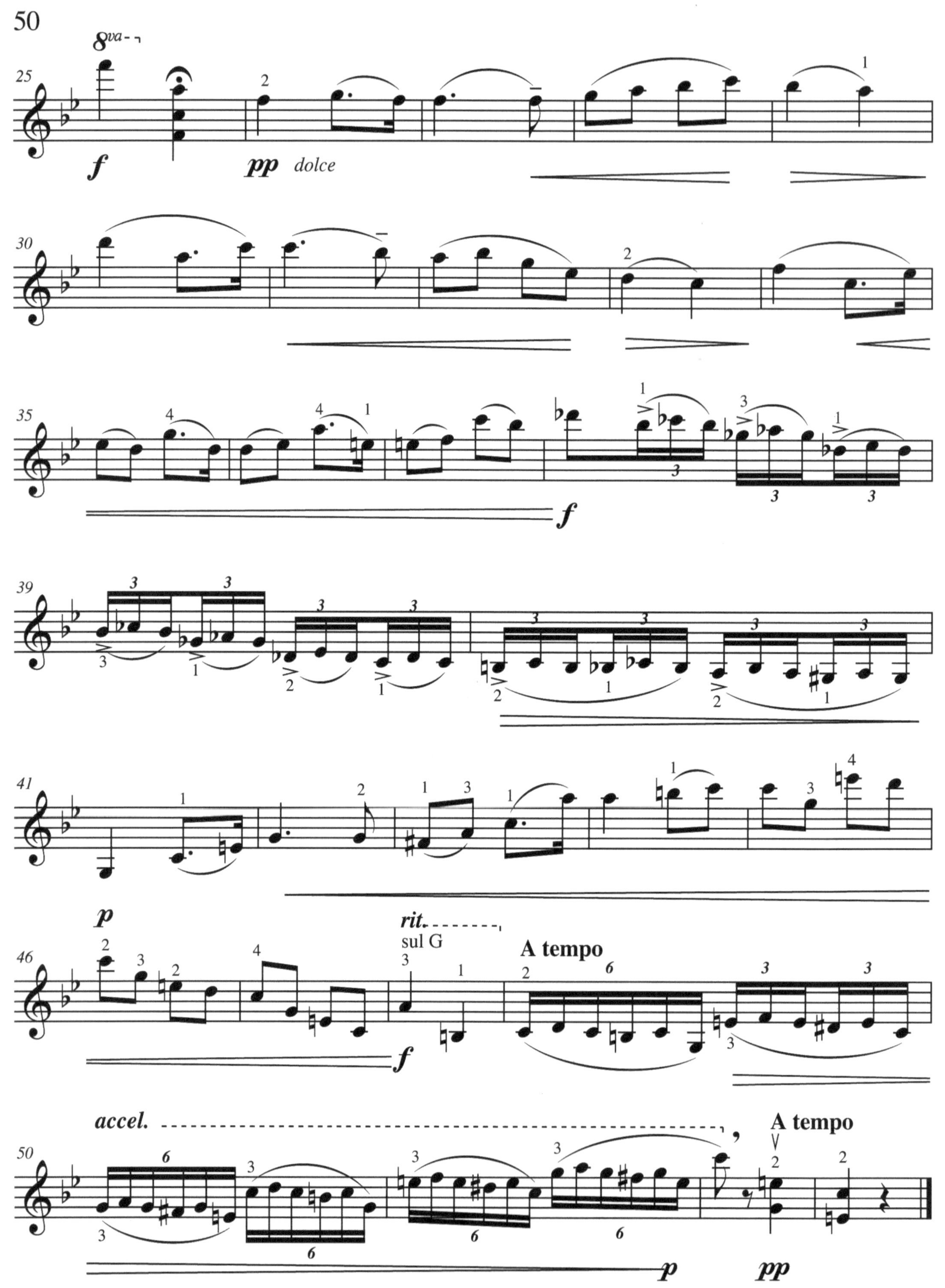
8va
f
pp dolce
f
p
rit.
sul G
A tempo
f
accel.
A tempo
p
pp

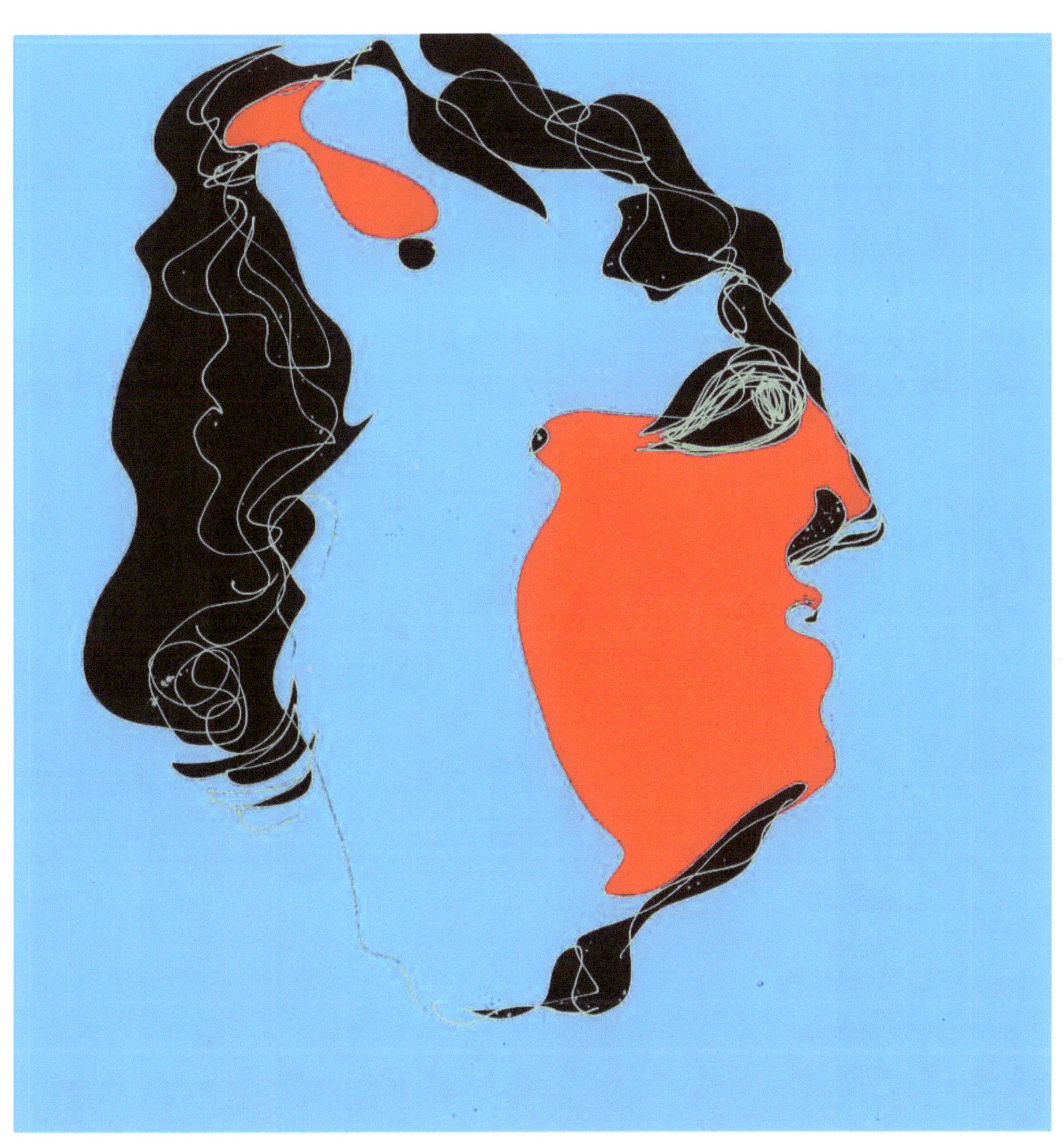

No. 14

Paganini

To Carolyn

XIV. Cadenza to First Movement of Concerto No. 1 by N. Paganini
"Paganini"

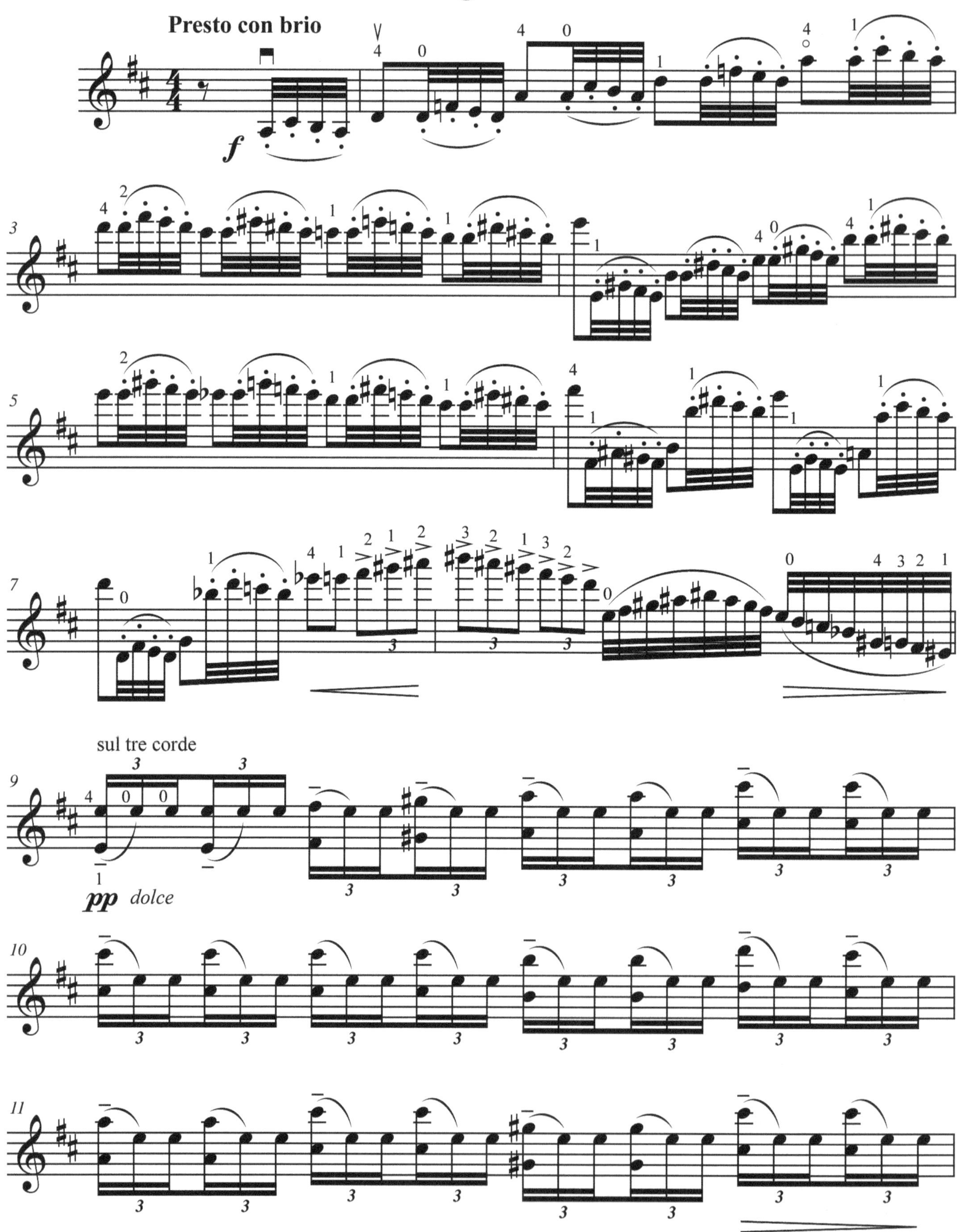

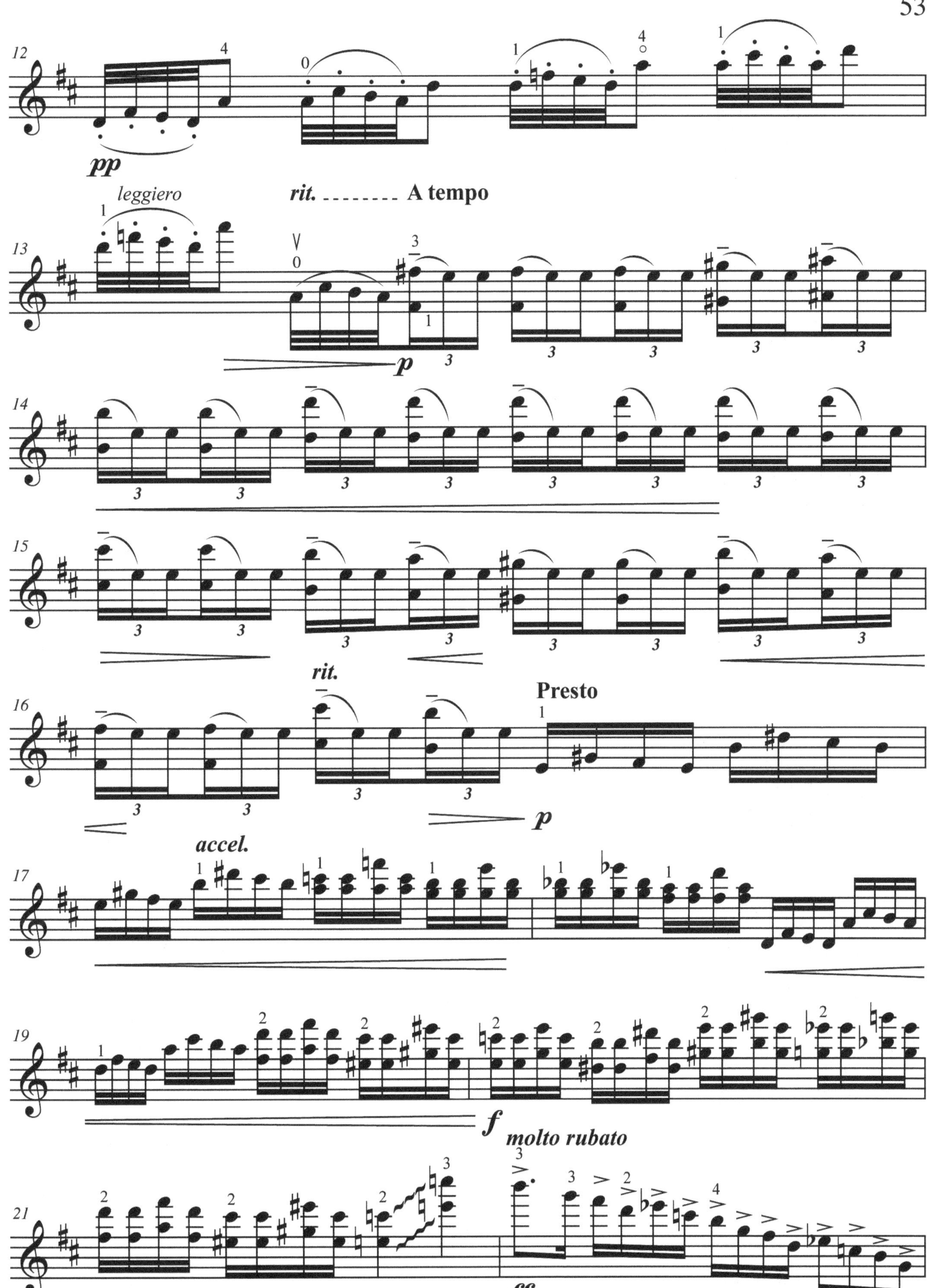

pp
leggiero
rit.
A tempo
p
rit.
Presto
p
accel.
f
molto rubato
ff

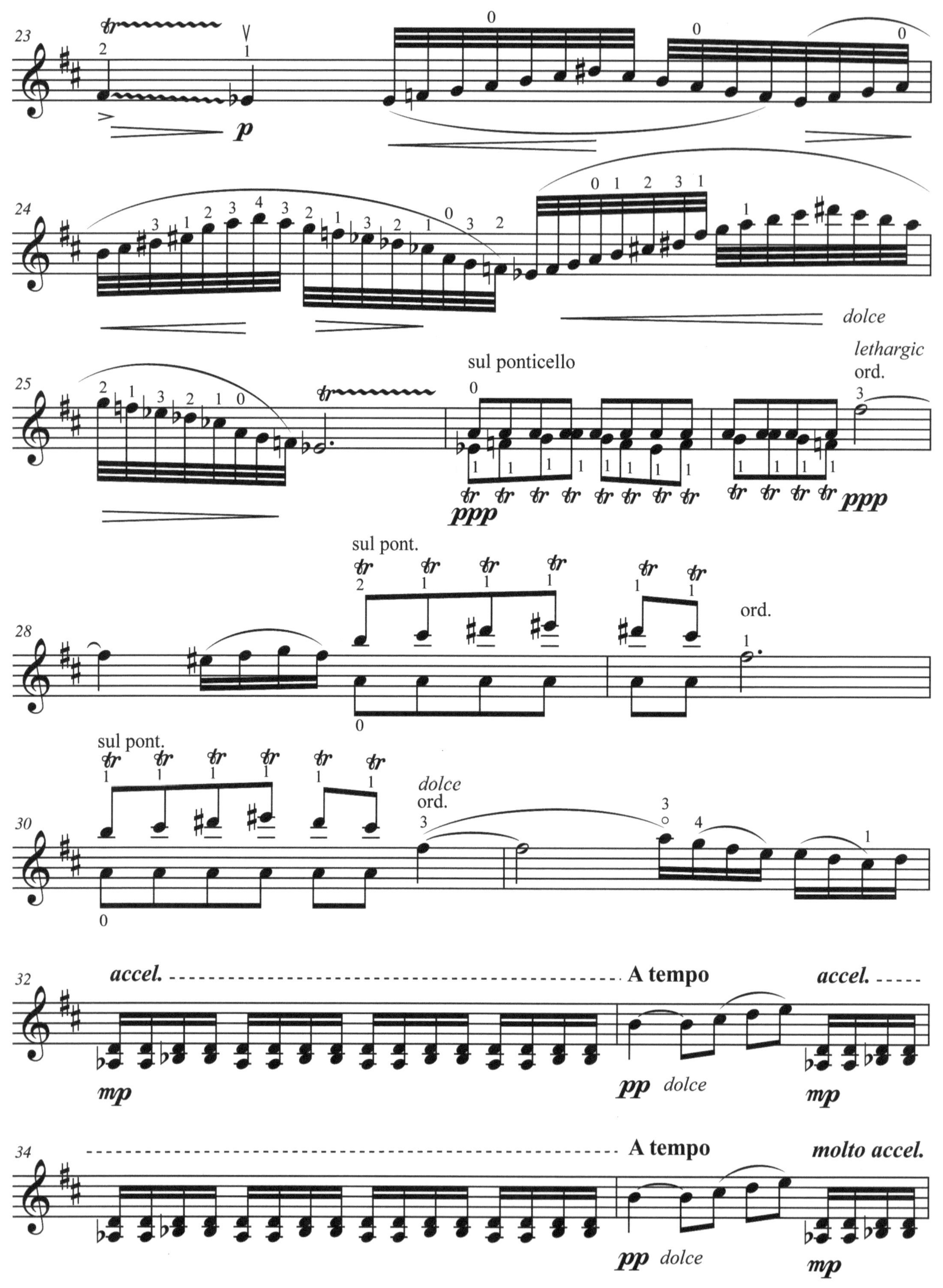

sul ponticello
lethargic
ord.
dolce
sul pont.
ord.
sul pont.
dolce
ord.
accel.
A tempo
accel.
pp dolce
mp
A tempo
molto accel.
pp dolce
mp

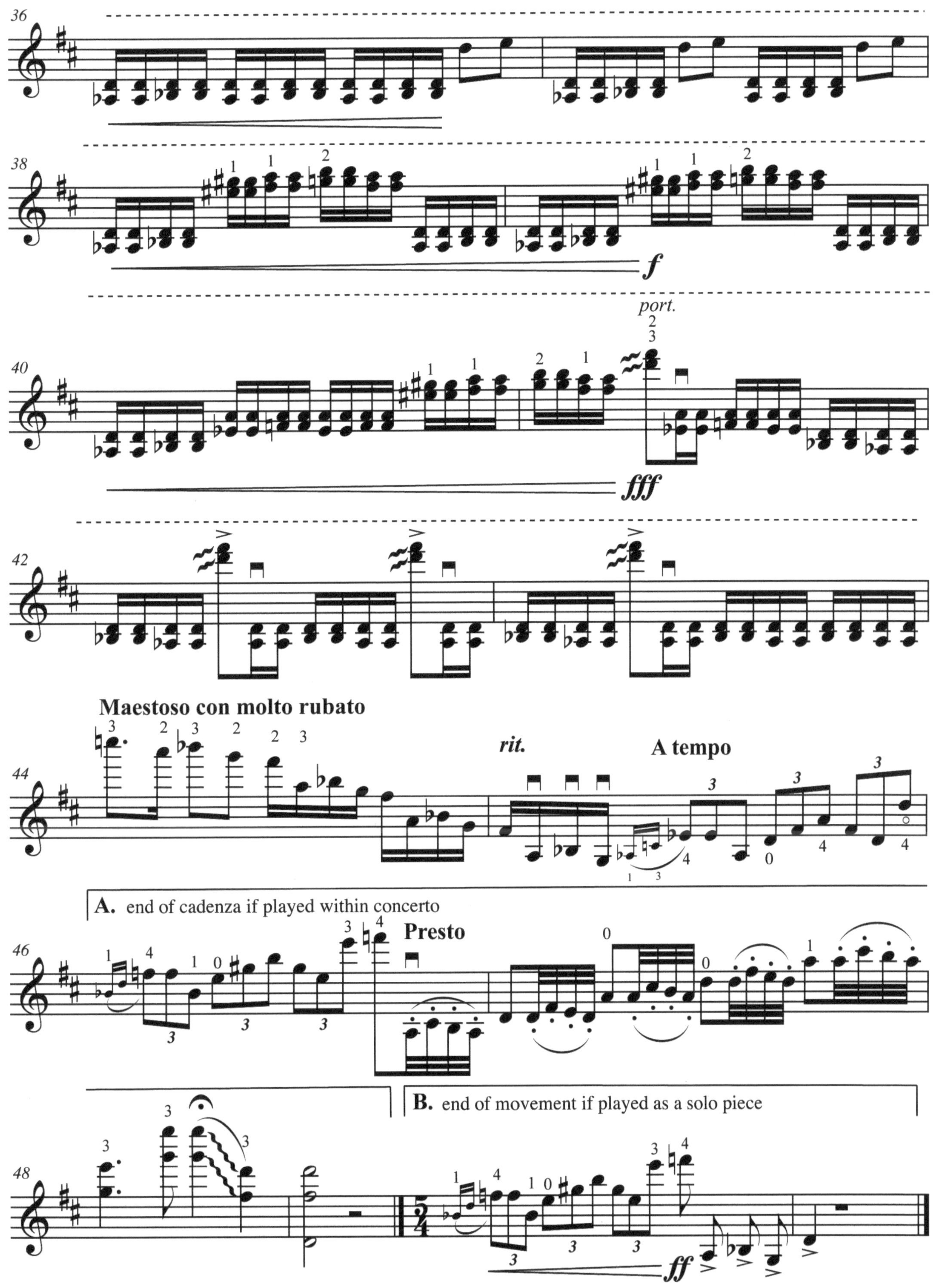

port.
fff
Maestoso con molto rubato
rit.
A tempo
A. end of cadenza if played within concerto
Presto
B. end of movement if played as a solo piece
ff

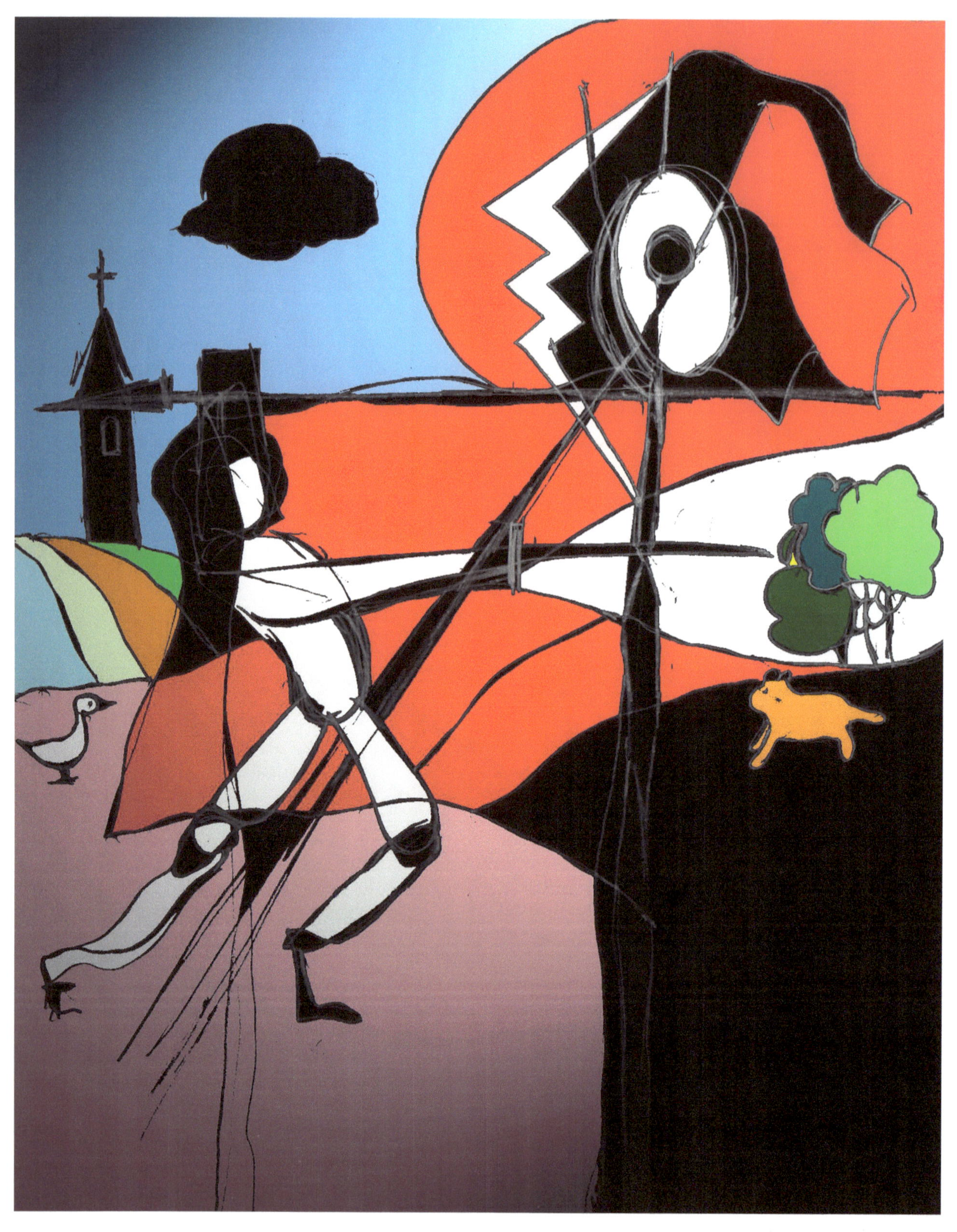

No. 15

Vieuxtemps

To I.T.

XV. Cadenza to First Movement of Concerto No. 5 by H. Vieuxtemps
"Vieuxtemps"

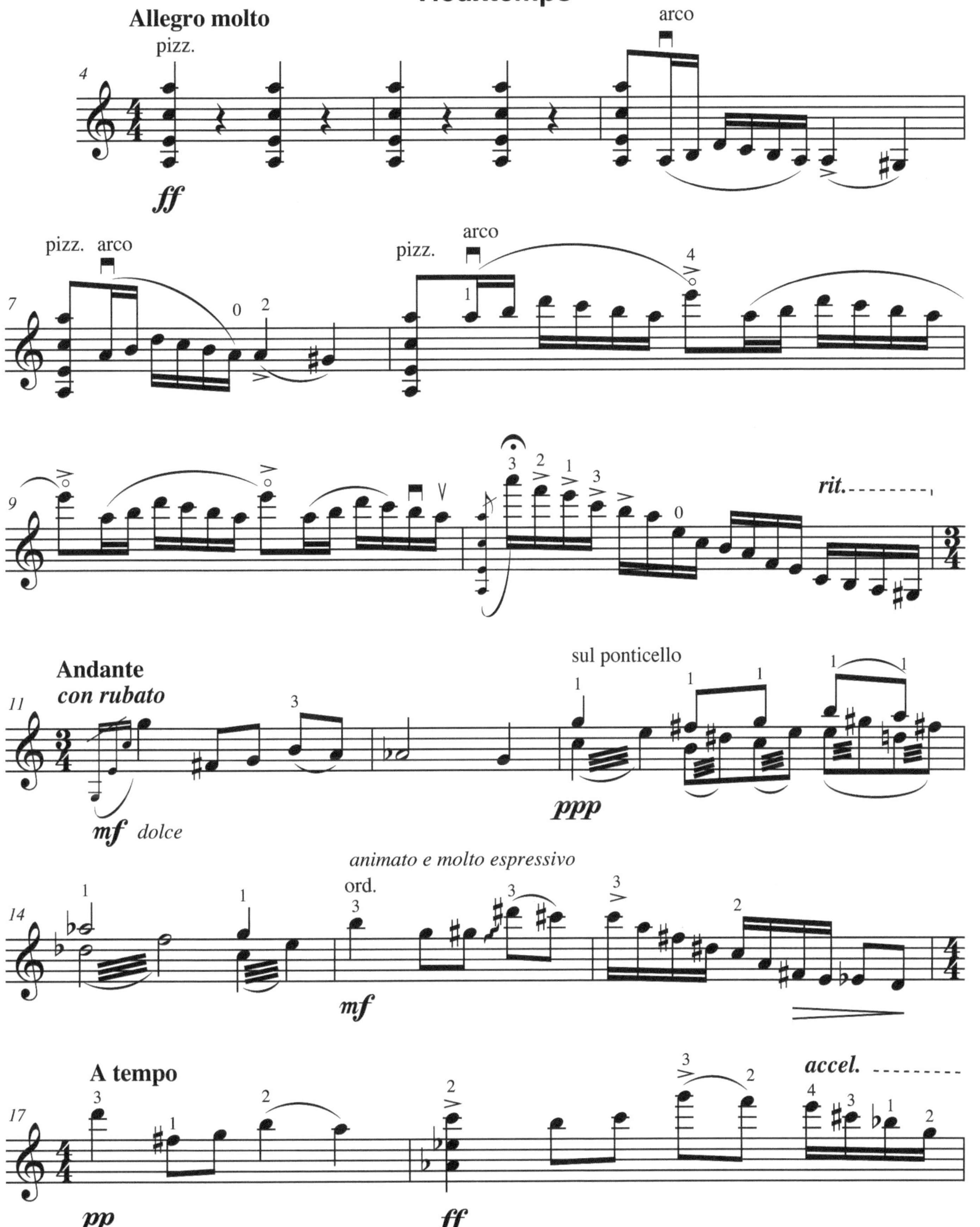

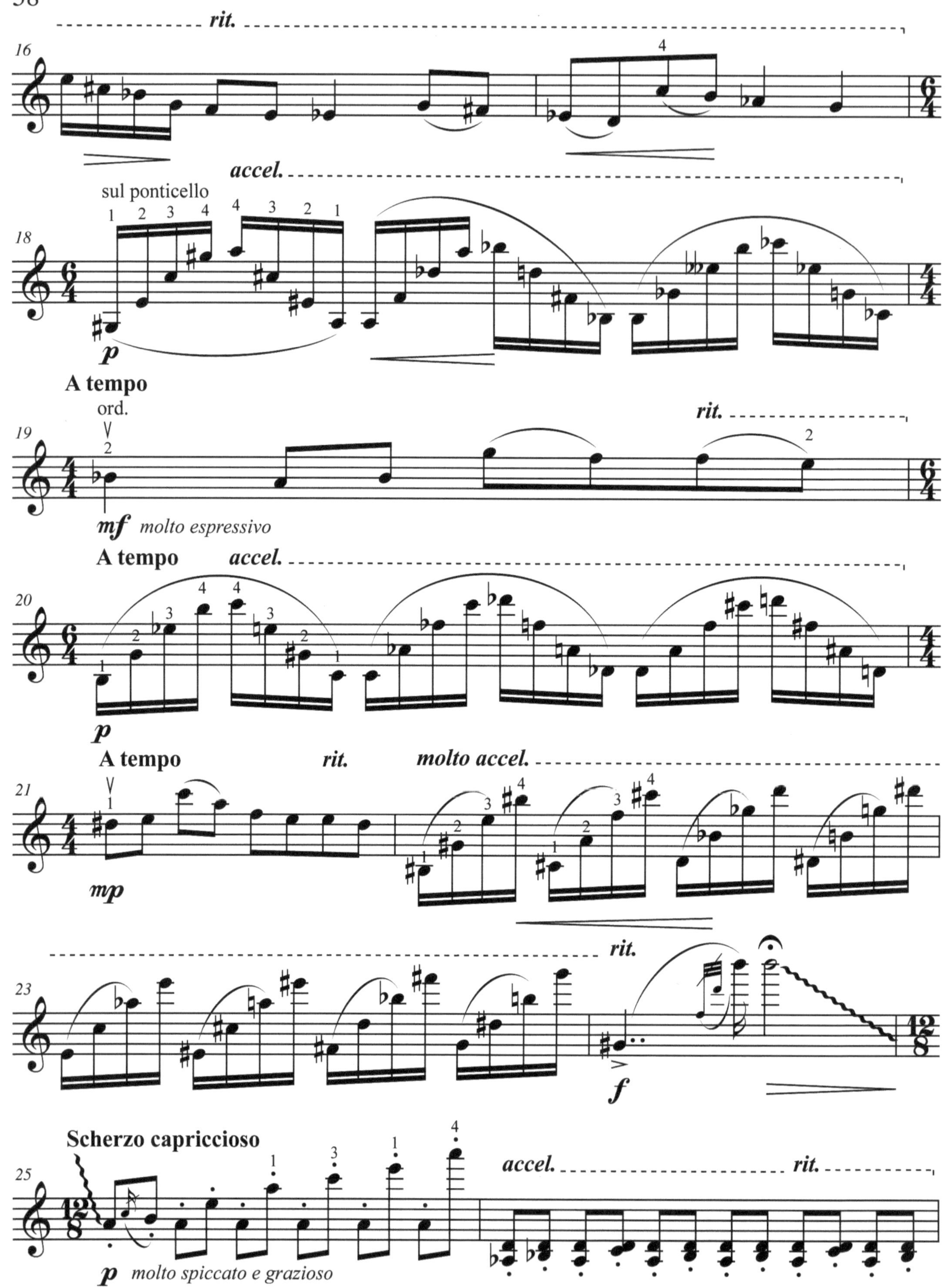
rit.
accel.
sul ponticello
A tempo
ord.
rit.
molto espressivo
A tempo
accel.
A tempo
rit.
molto accel.
rit.
Scherzo capriccioso
molto spiccato e grazioso
accel.
rit.

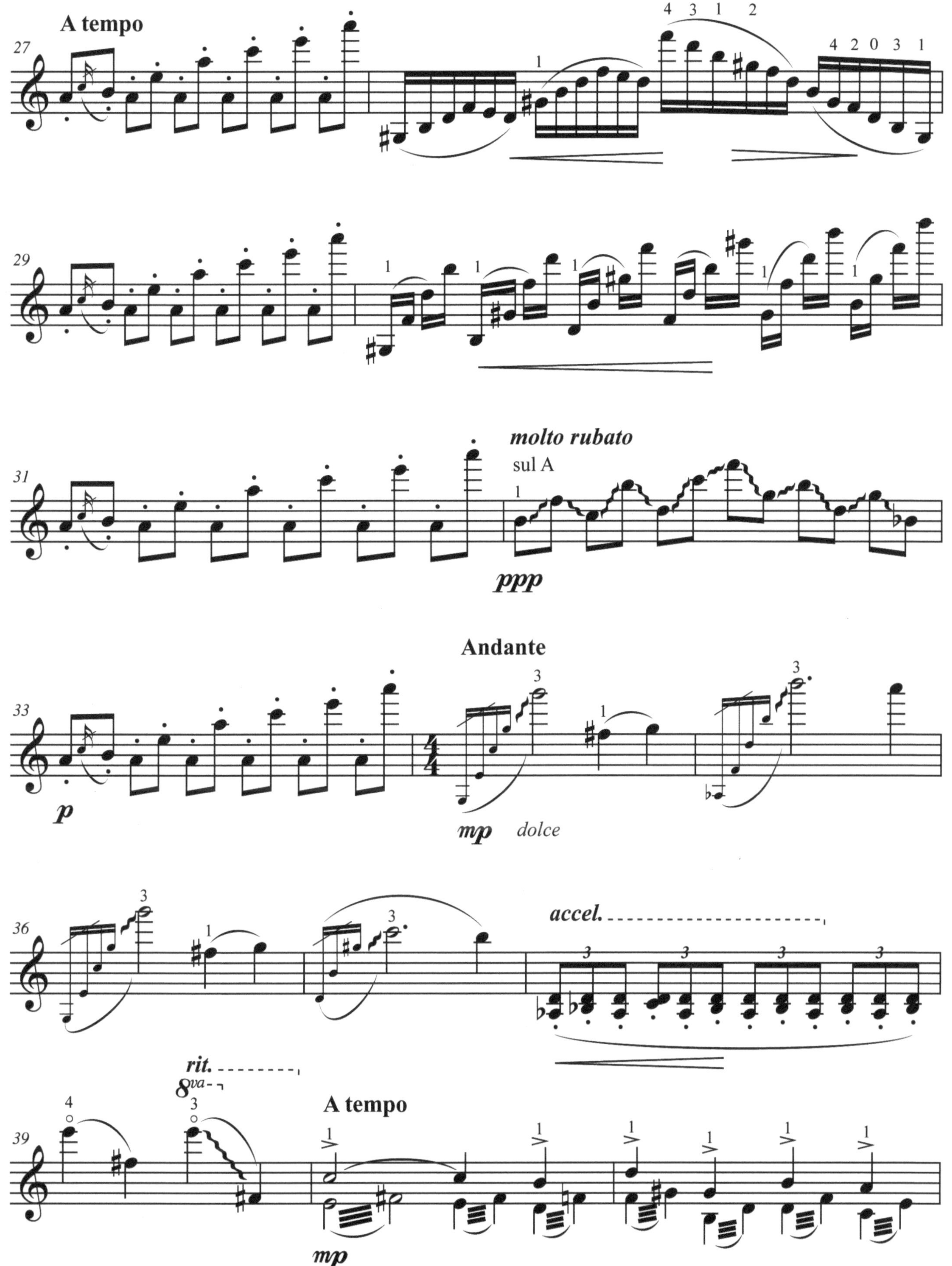
A tempo
molto rubato
sul A
ppp
Andante
p
mp
dolce
accel.
rit.
8va
A tempo
mp

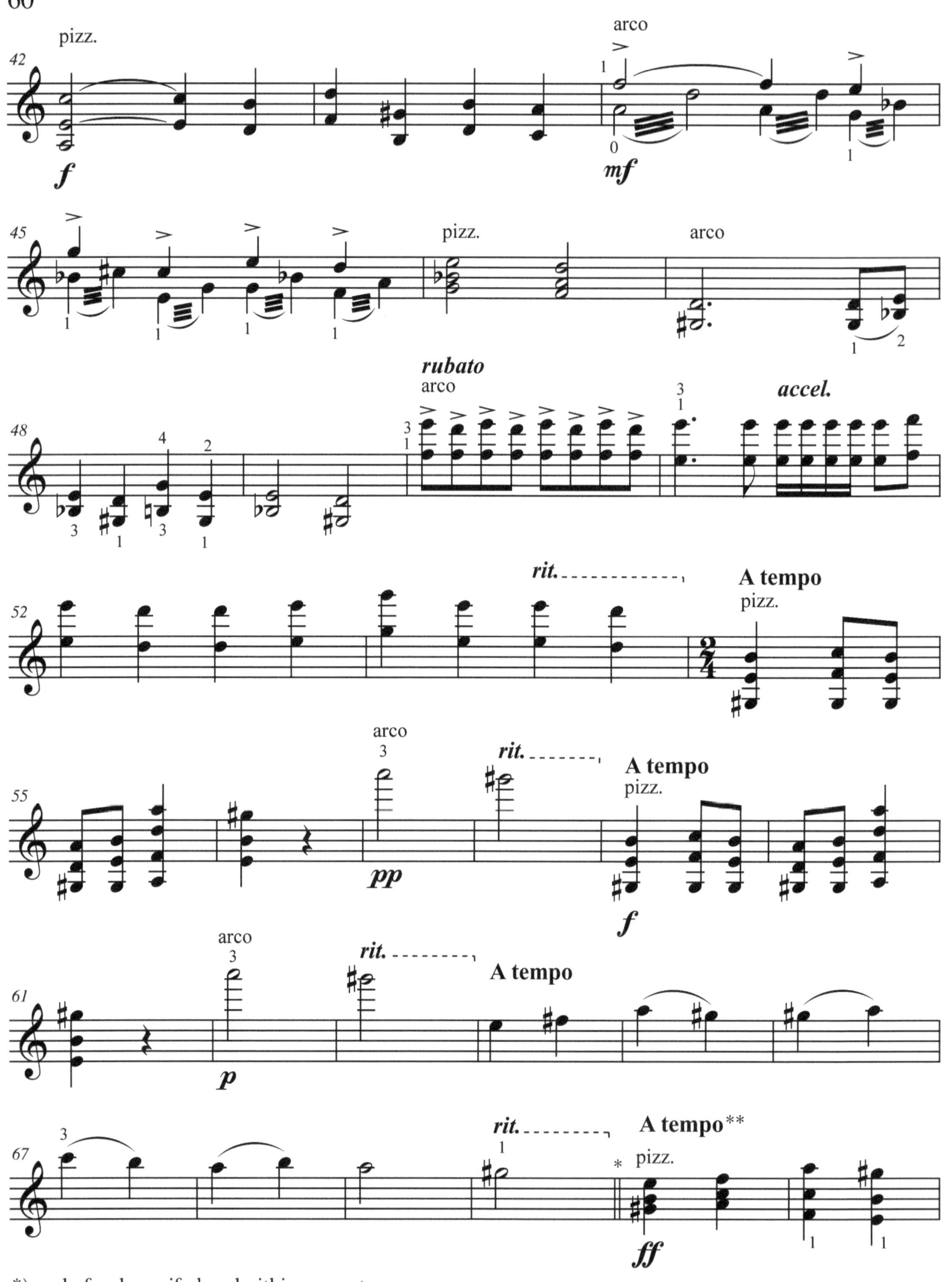

*) end of cadenza if played within concerto
**) Coda, if performed as a solo piece

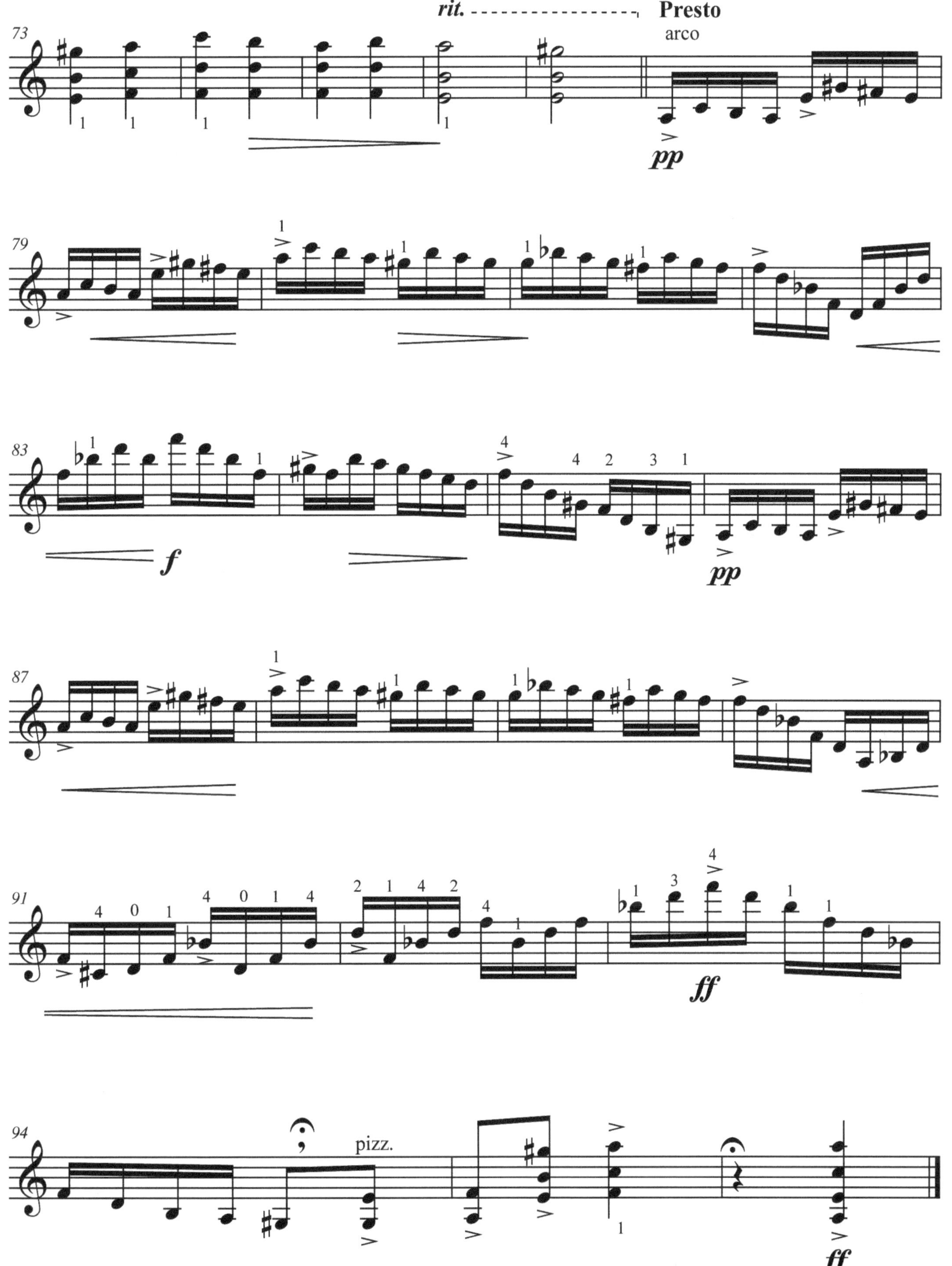
rit.
Presto
arco
pp
f
pp
ff
pizz.
ff

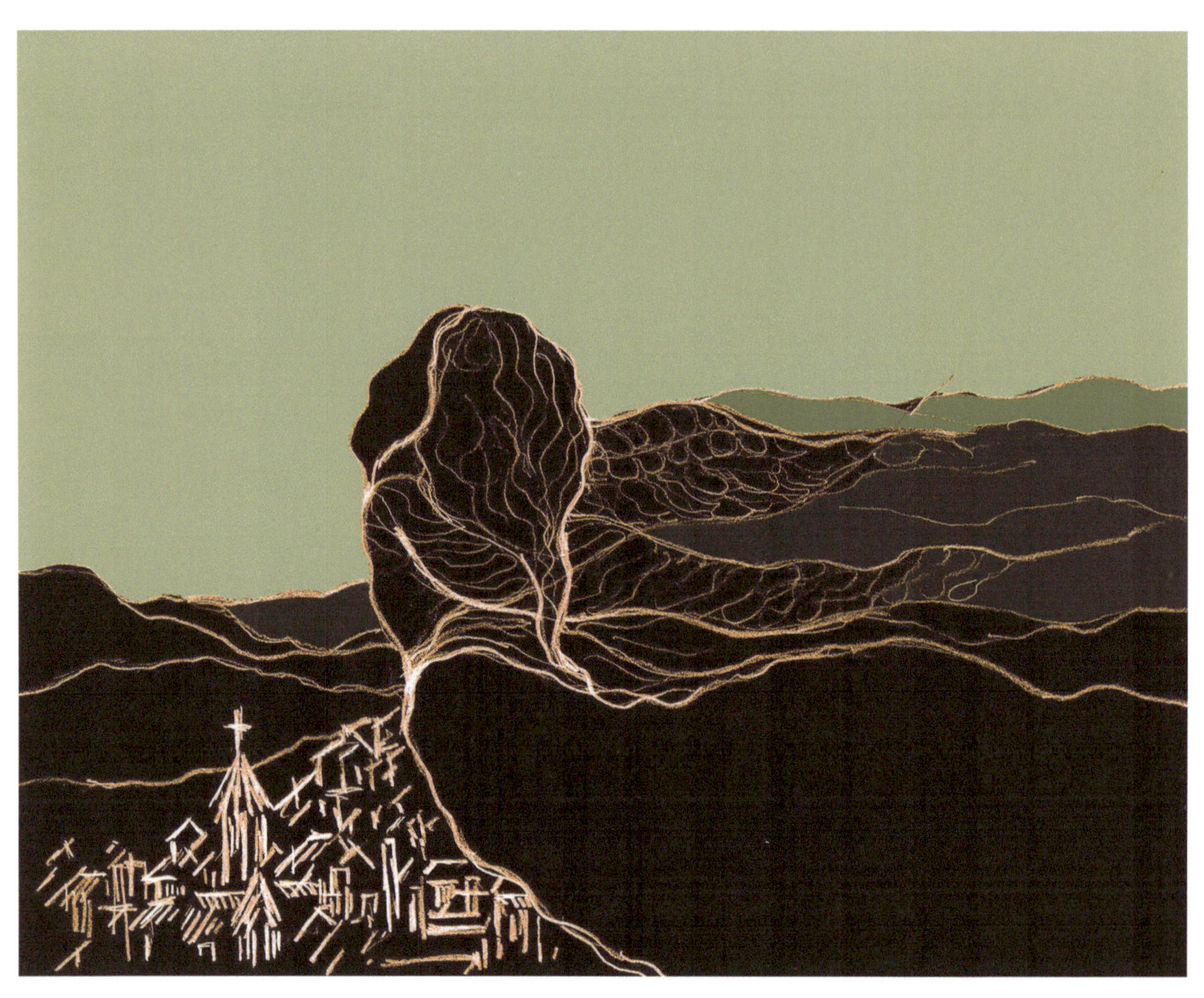

No. 16
Cadenza to the Third Movement
of Concerto by L. v. Beethoven
Awakening

XVI. Cadenza to the Third Movement of Beethoven's Concerto for Violin
"Awakening"

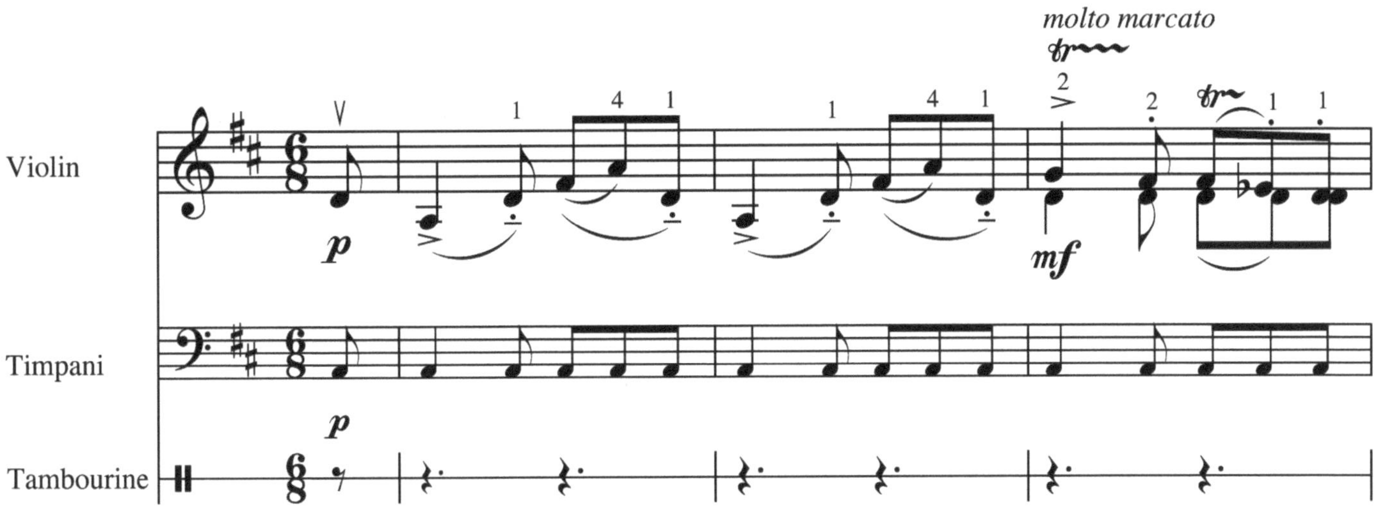

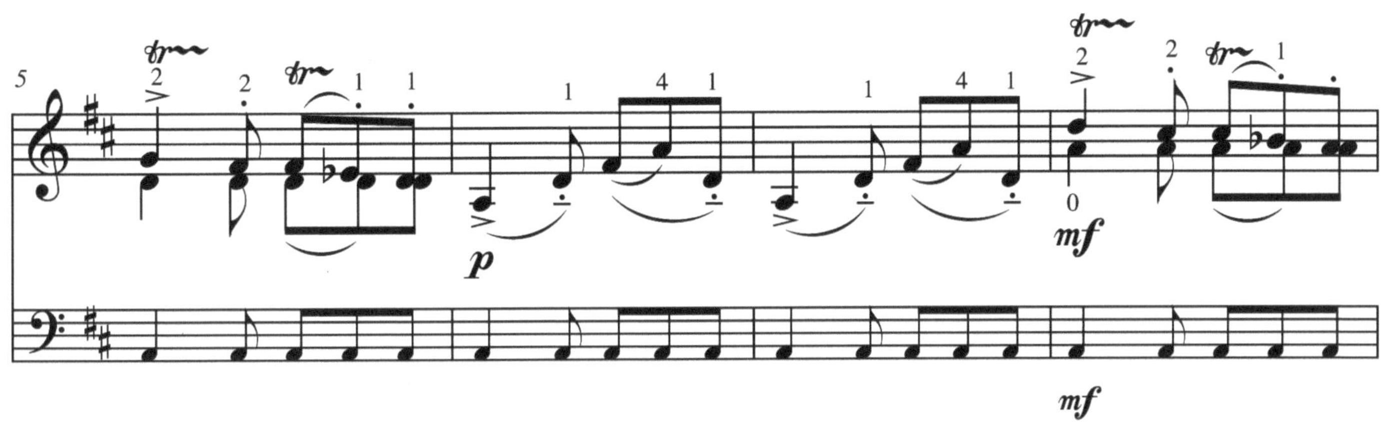

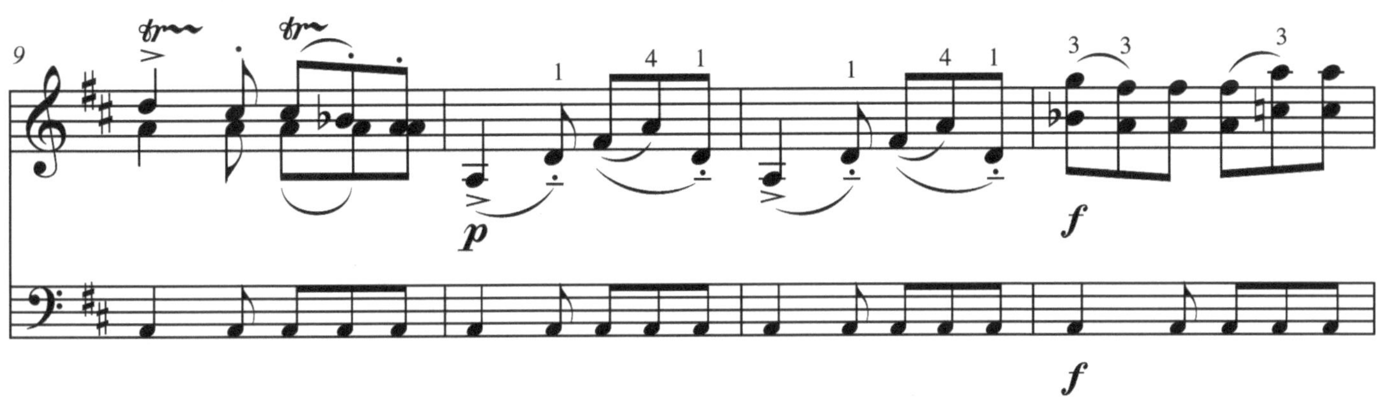

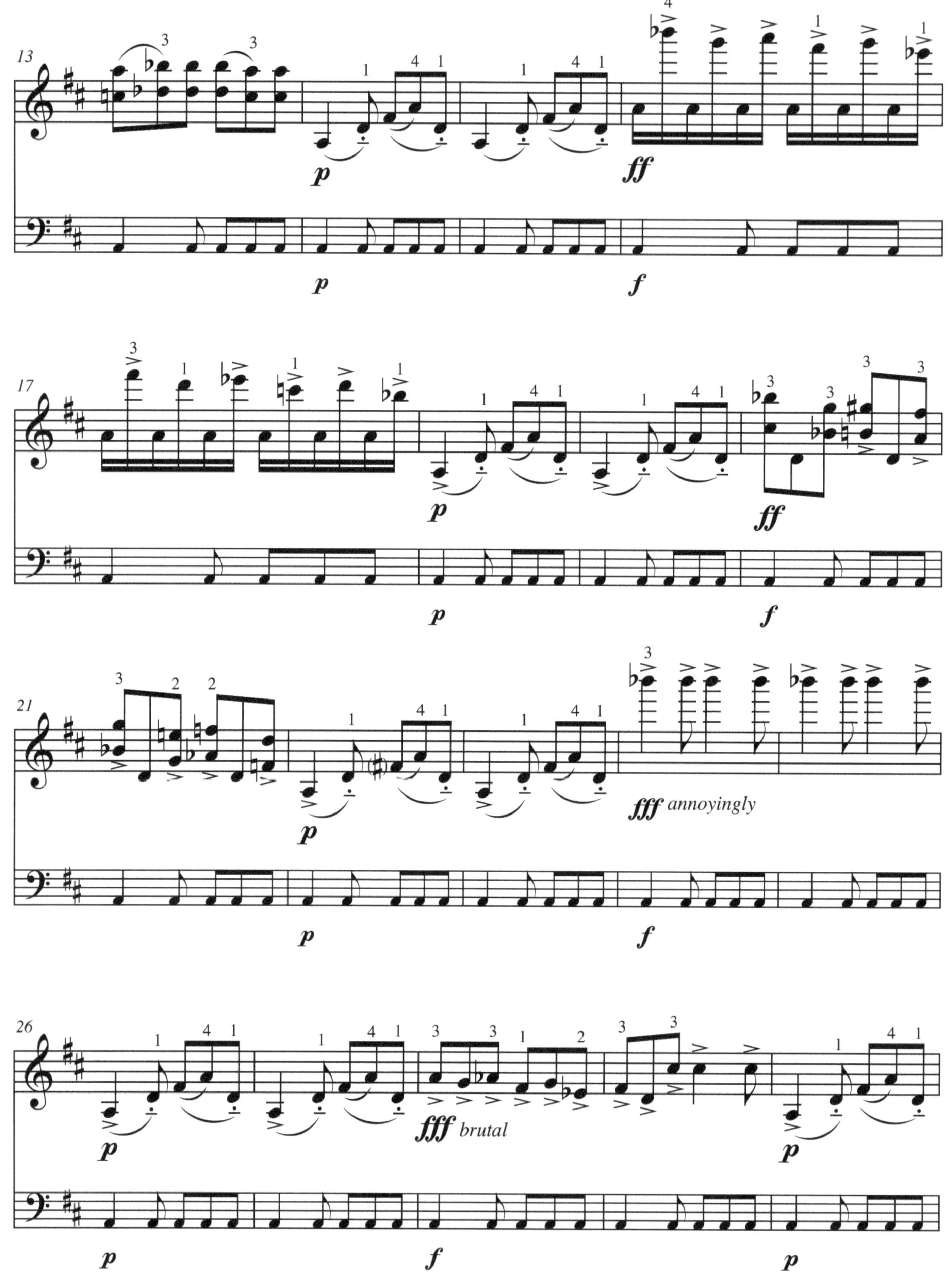

13
17
21
26
fff annoyingly
fff brutal

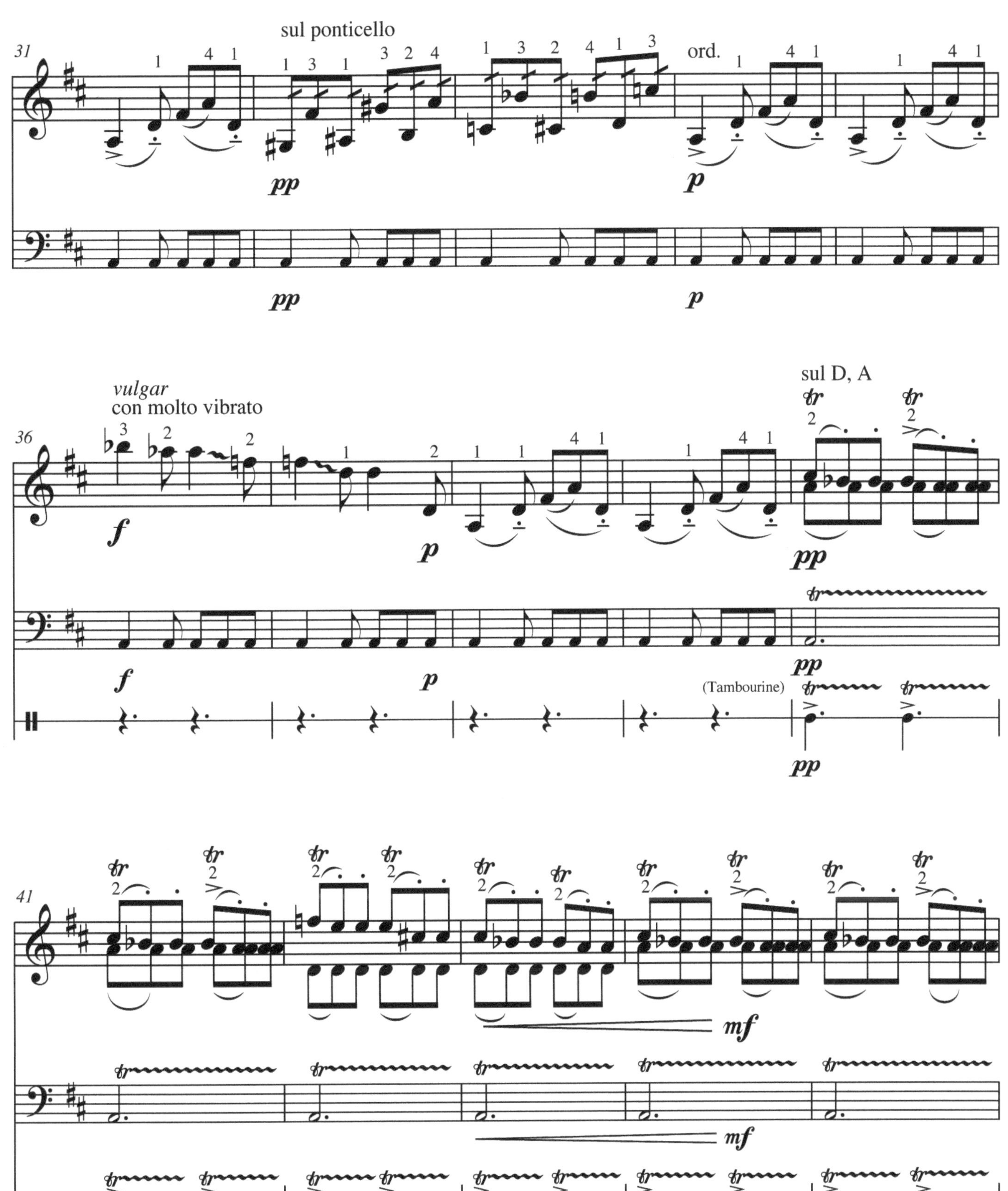
31
sul ponticello
ord.
pp
p
36
vulgar
con molto vibrato
sul D, A
f
p
pp
(Tambourine)
41
mf

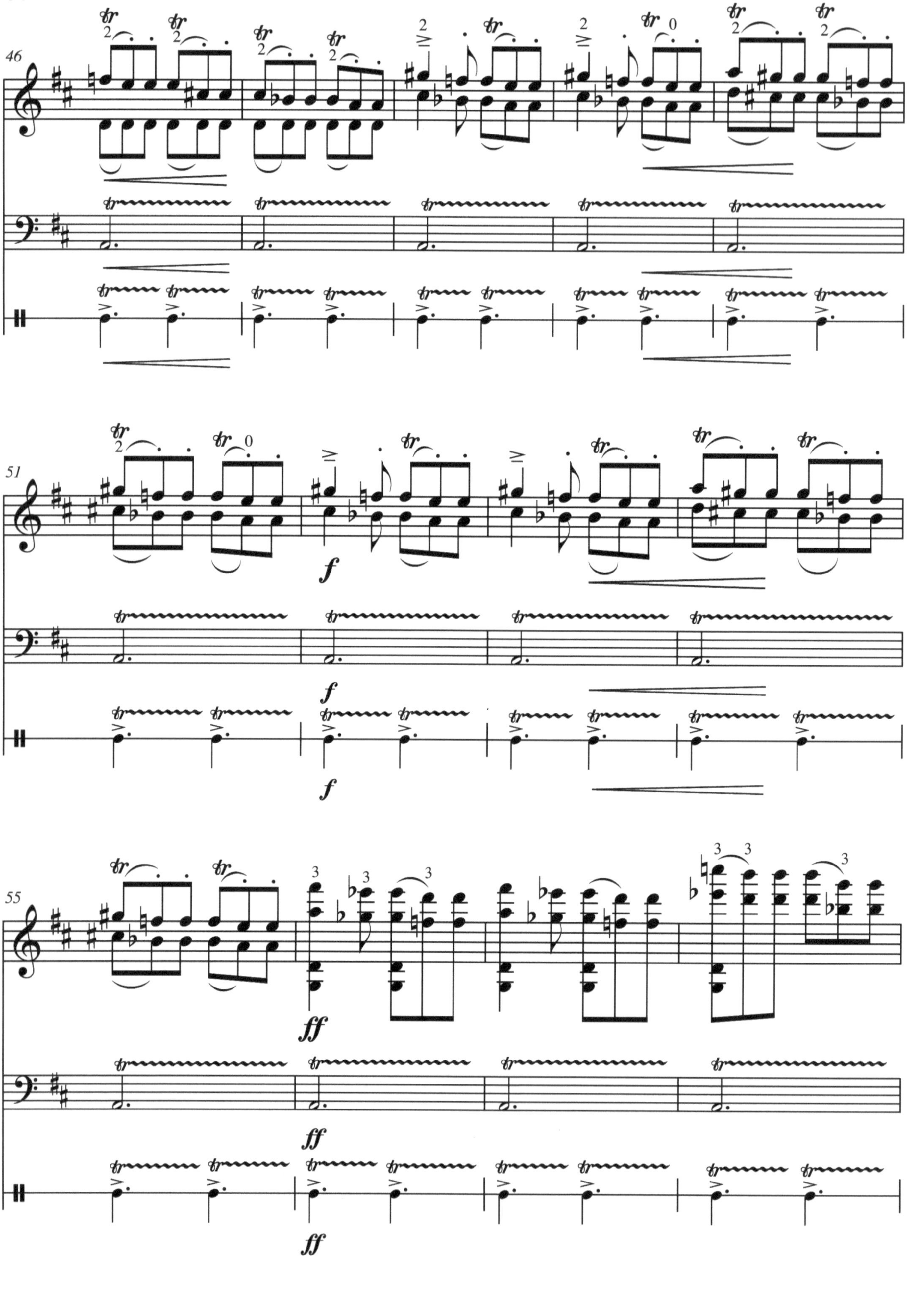

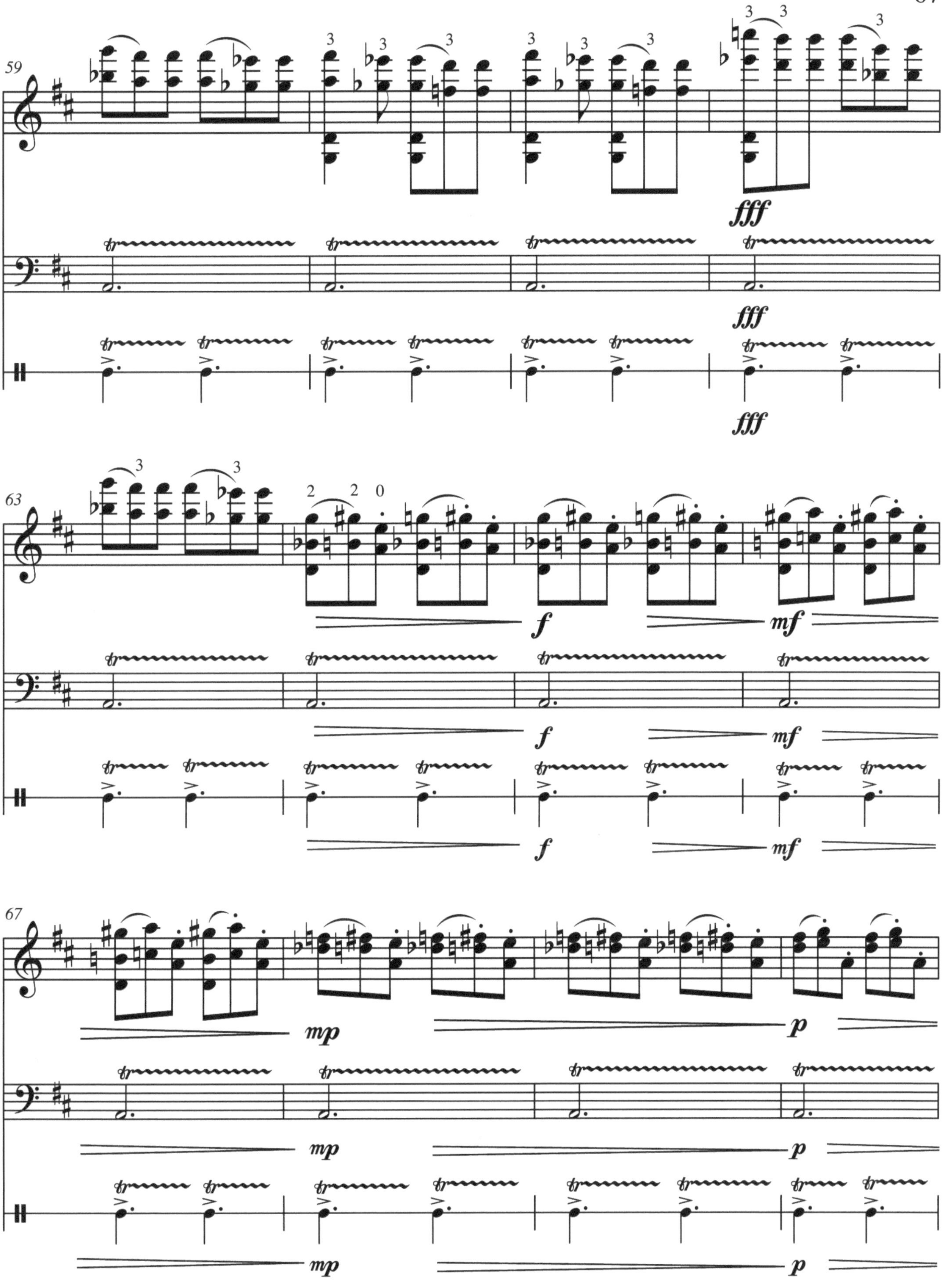
59
fff
fff
fff
63
f
mf
f
mf
f
mf
67
mp
p
mp
p
mp
p

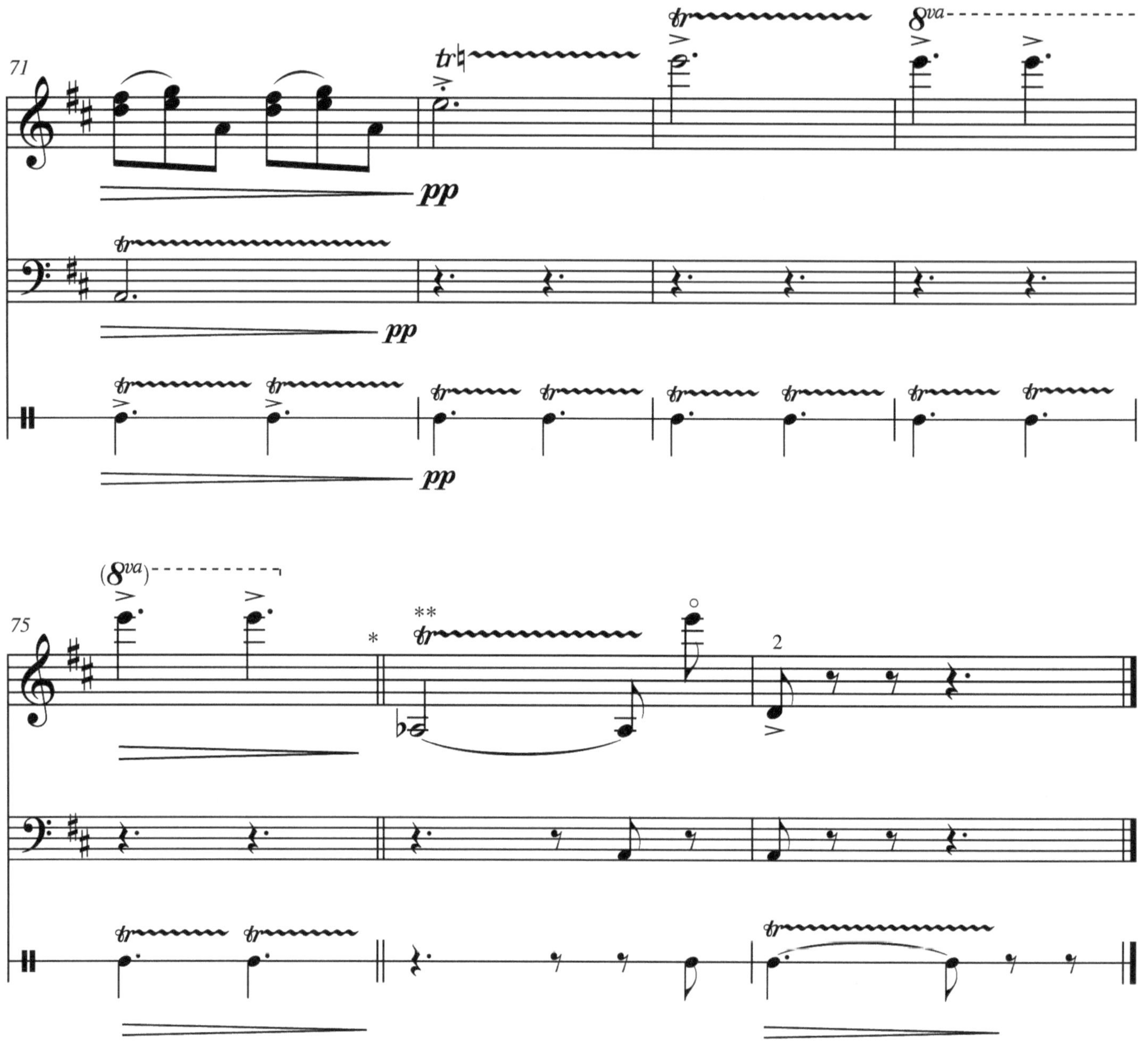

*) end of cadenza if played within concerto
**) ending if performed as a solo piece

Michael Tseitlin's Publications:

Three Cadenzas to Beethoven Violin Concerto, Op. 1

Overture "750", Op. 2, Orchestral Score

"Circus 1937", Op. 3 bis Fantasy for Violin and Piano

"Circus 1937" One Act Ballet, Op. 3. Orchestral Score

16 Caprices for Solo Violin, Op. 4

"Schumann" Op. 5, Fantasy for Violin and Piano

"How to Play Violin and Love It Too" Series

Incredible Adventures of Little Slonik. 22 pieces for Violin and Piano, Op. 6

Incredible Adventures of Little Zaika,
Three Concertinos in Style of Mendelssohn, Haydn, and Bach, Op. 7

Slonik Goes to Animal Olympics. 16 pieces for Violin and Piano, Op. 8

Incredible Adventures of Little Zaika in Pumpkinland.
12 pieces for Violin and Piano, Op. 9

Violin Cookbook "How to Play Violin and Love It Too". Method Book

Duo "Who Are You?" for Violin and Cello, Op. 10

Trio: Intermezzo and 10 Waltzes "Everyday life and Midnight Clock"
For Violin, Cello and Piano, Op. 11

Quartet "Murder on the Saint's Day (Imenini)" for Two Violins, Cello and Double Bass, Op. 12

Two Violin Transcriptions: "Widmung" and "Samson and Delilah", Op. 14

Dance Lesson (Urok Tanza), Op. 15, Duo for Violin and Cello

Quartet in One, Op. 16 for Violin Solo

Passacaglia and Fanfares, Op. 17 for Violin, Percussion and Piano

Six Variations on Original Theme in Style of Haydn and Two Dreams for Violin and Chamber Orchestra, Op. 18

String Quintet "Marusia" for Two Violins, Viola or Clarinet, Cello and Double Bass, Op. 19

Lullaby for Solo Violin in 4 voices, Op. 20

Sonata for Violin and Piano, Op. 21

Trio for Violin, Clarinet and Piano, Op. 22

To find out more about Michael Tseitlin art go to www.MichaelTseitlin.com

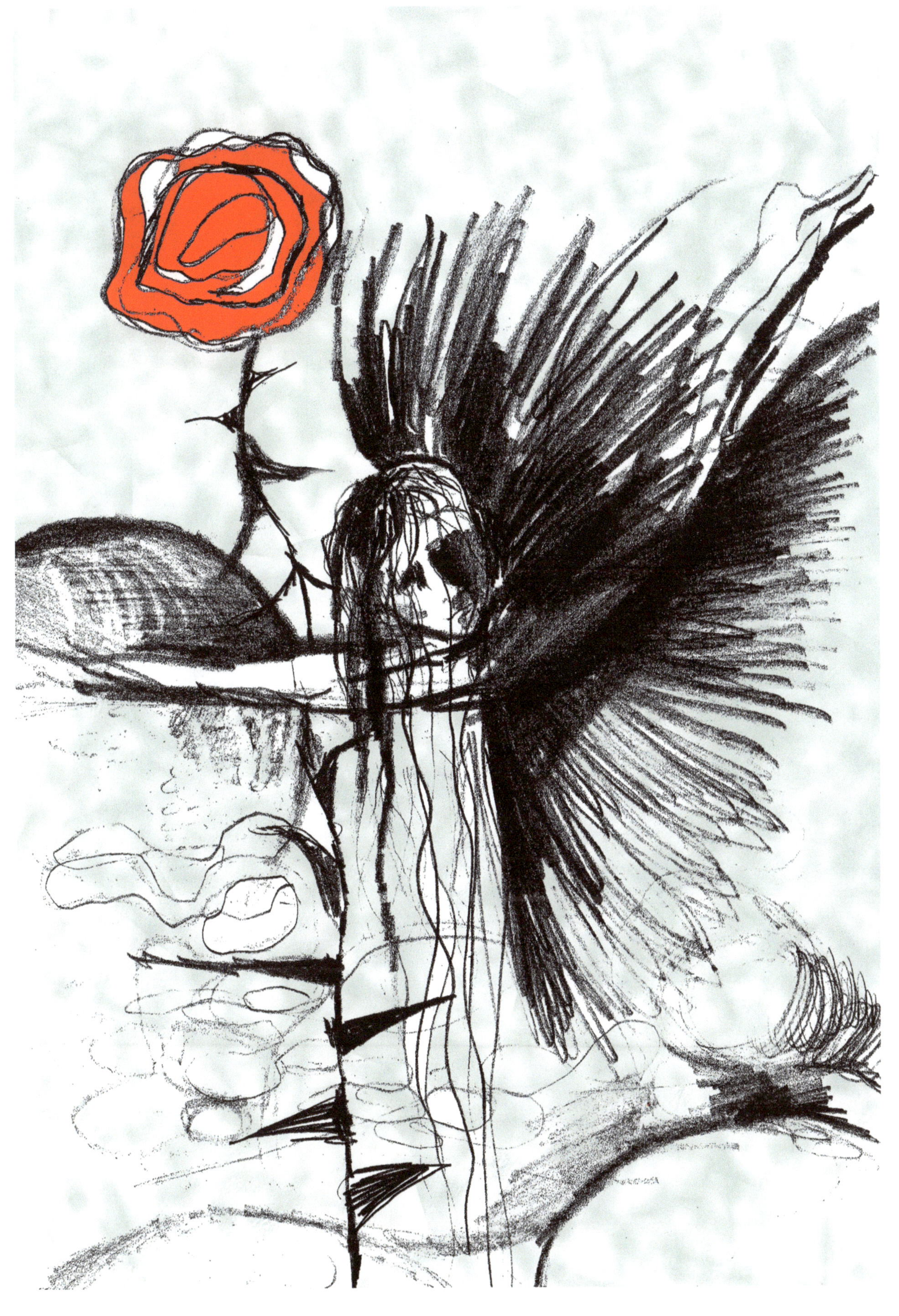

The Rose

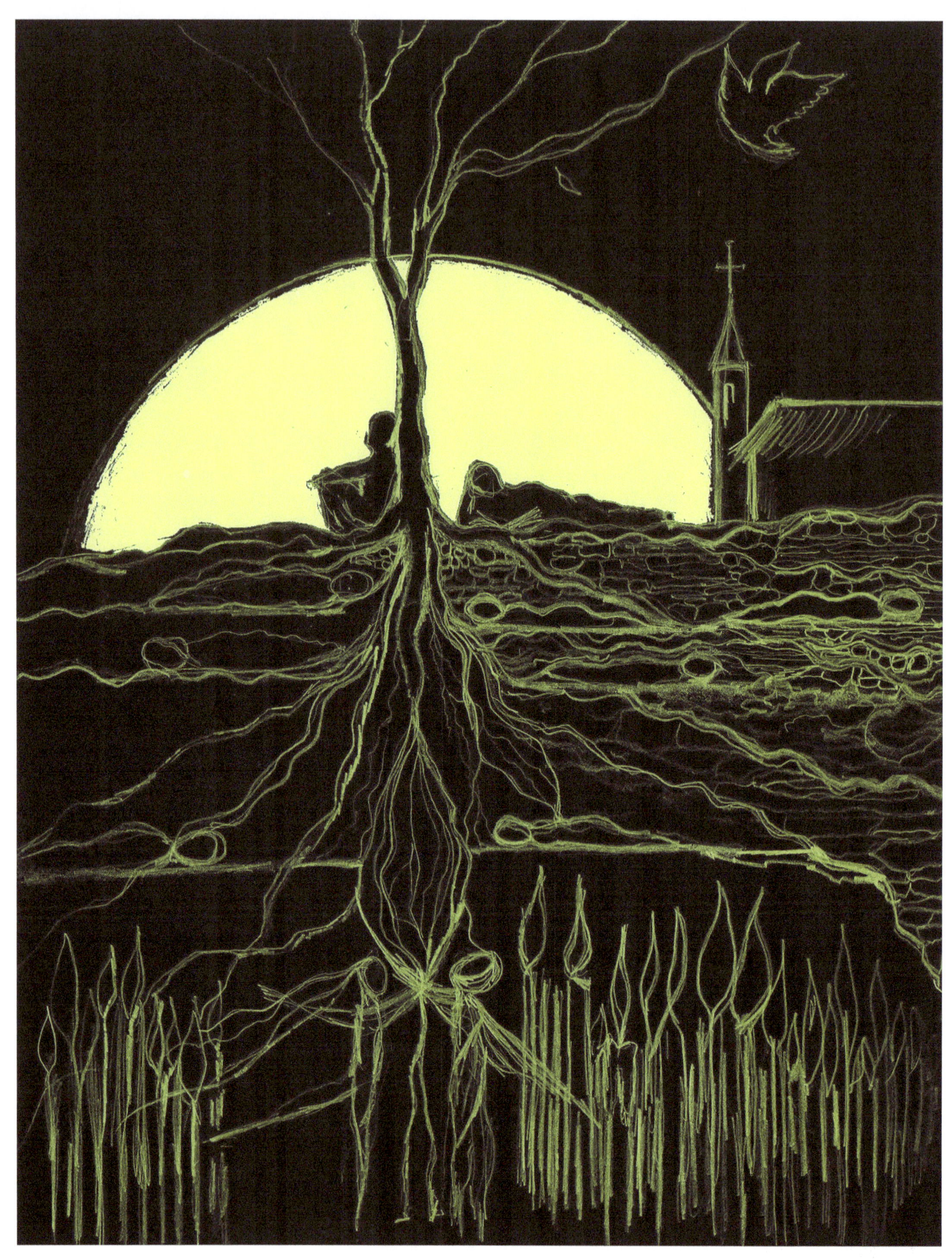

Green Night

Other publication By Michael Tseitlin

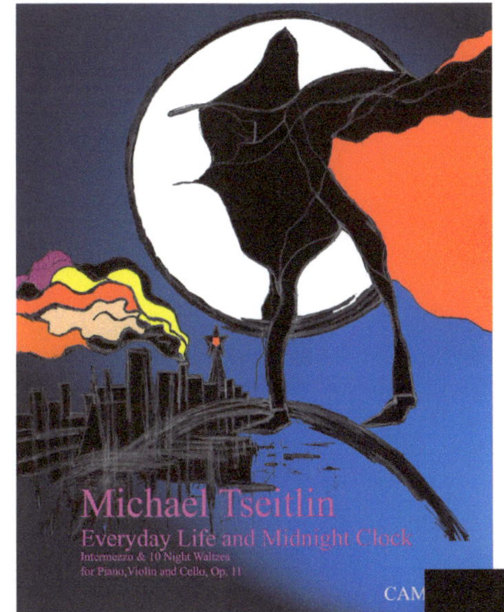

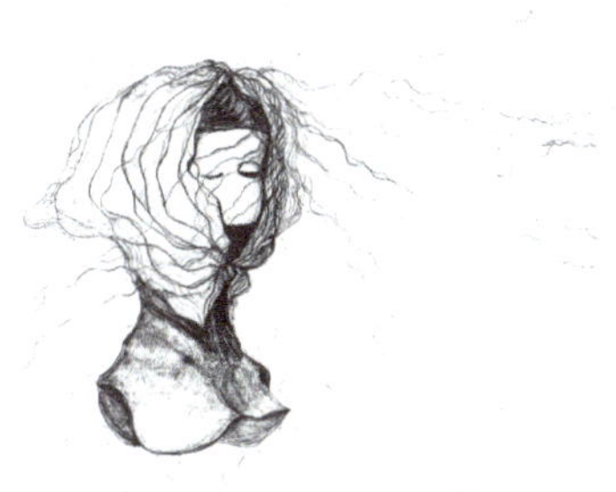

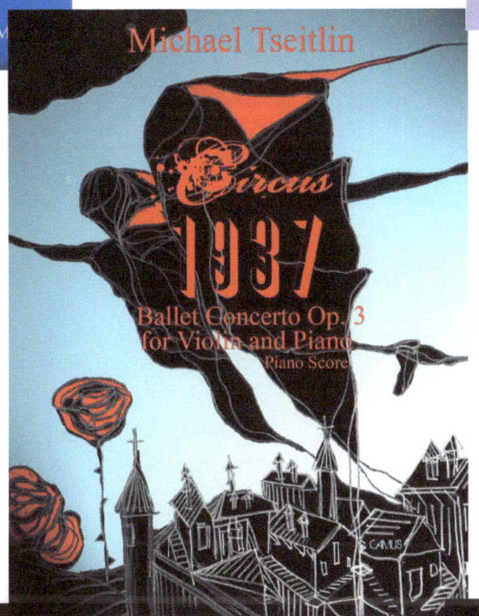

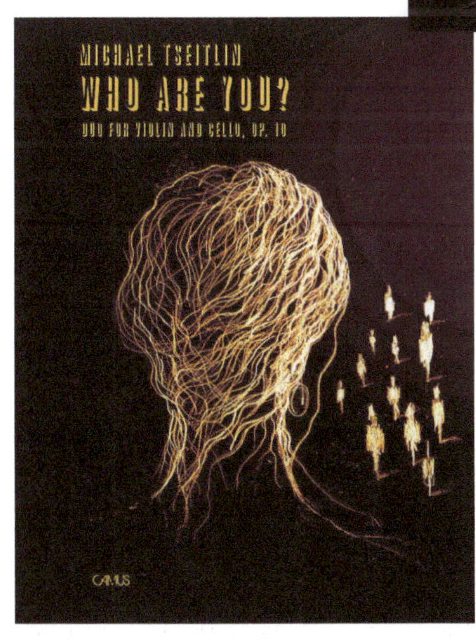

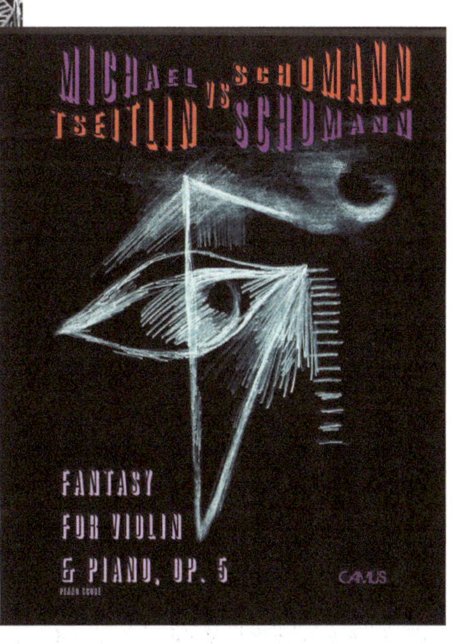

Music by Michael Tseitlin:

- Three Cadenzas to Beethoven Violin Concerto, Op. 1
- Overture "750", Op. 2, Orchestral Score
- "Circus 1937", Op. 3bis Fantasy for Violin and Piano
- "Circus 1937" One Act Ballet, Op. 3. Orchestral Score
- 16 Caprices for Solo Violin, Op. 4
- "Schumann" Op. 5, Fantasy for Violin and Piano
- "Incredible Adventures of Little Slonik", 22 pieces for Violin and Piano, Op. 6
- Three Concertinos in Style of Mendelssohn, Haydn, and Bach, Op. 7
- "Slonik Goes to Animal Olympics", 16 pieces for Violin and Piano, Op. 8
- "Incredible Adventures of Little Zaika in Pumpkinland",
  12 pieces for Violin and Piano, Op. 9
- Duo "Who Are You?" for Violin and Cello, Op. 10
- Trio: "Everyday life and Midnight Clock"Intermezzo and 10 Night Waltzes
  For Piano, Violin and Cello, Op. 11
- Quartet "Murder on the Saint's Day" for Two Violins, Cello and Double Bass, Op. 12
- Two Violin Transcriptions: "Widmung" and "Samson and Delilah", Op. 14
- Dance Lesson (Urok Tanza), Op. 15, Duo for Violin and Cello
- Quartet in One, Op. 16 for Violin Solo
- Passacaglia and Fanfares, Op. 17 for Violin, Percussion and Piano
- Six Variations on Original Theme in Style of Haydn and Two Dreams for Violin and Chamber Orchestra, Op. 18
- Quintet "Marusia" for Two Violins, Viola or Clarinet, Cello and Double Bass, Op. 19
- Lullaby for Solo Violin in 4 voices, Op. 20
- Sonata for Violin and Piano, Op. 21
- Trio for Violin, Clarinet and Piano, Op. 22
- "Murder of Carmen" Fantasy for Violin and Piano, Op. 23
- "Last Night of Samson and Delilah" Fantasy for Violin and Piano, Op. 24
- "Prelude, Three Dances, and Wedding Procession of Cinderella"
  Fantasy for 2 Violins and Piano, Op. 25

Books by Michael and Irina Tseitlin

- "How to Play Violin and Love It Too" Series
  Violin Cookbook "How to Play Violin and Love It Too". Method Book
- Incredible Adventures of Little Slonik
- Slonik goes to Animal Olympics
- Incredible Adventures of Little Slonik on the Day Before Christmas
- Cinderella and her Father
- How the World Works. Stories about Little Boy Who New How
- Power of 1 and Only
- Little Greedy Bedside Stories
- "Circus 1937" novel

To find out more about Michael and Irina Tseitlin art go to www.MichaelTseitlin.com

www.ingramcontent.com/pod-product-compliance
Lightning Source LLC
LaVergne TN
LVHW070139110826
845147LV00002B/291
* 9 7 8 0 5 5 7 1 2 5 1 5 9 *